Suffering and Psychology

Suffering and Psychology challenges modern psychology's concentration almost exclusively on eradicating pain, suffering, and their causes. Modern psychology and psychotherapy are motivated in part by a humane and compassionate desire to relieve many kinds of human suffering. However, they have concentrated almost exclusively on eradicating pain, suffering, and their causes. In doing so psychology perpetuates modern ideologies of individual human freedom and expanding instrumental control that foster worthy ideals but are distinctly limited and by themselves quite self-defeating and damaging in the long run.

This book explores theoretical commitments and cultural ideals that deter the field of psychology from facing and dealing credibly with inescapable human limitations and frailties, and with unavoidable suffering, pain, loss, heartbreak, and despair. Drawing on both secular and spiritual points of view, this book seeks to recover ideals of character and compassion and to illuminate the possibility of what Jonathan Sacks terms "transforming suffering" rather than seeking mainly to eliminate, anesthetize, or defy these dark and difficult aspects of the human condition.

Suffering and Psychology will be of interest to academic and professional psychologists.

Frank C. Richardson is Professor of Educational Psychology (emeritus) at the University of Texas, Austin. He is author or coeditor of several books, including *Re-envisioning Psychology*, *Critical Thinking About Psychology*, and the *Routledge International Handbook of Theoretical and Philosophical Psychology* and the author of many articles and chapters in theoretical psychology and the philosophy of social science. His current interests include topics in psychology and religion. He is a past president of the Society for Theoretical and Philosophical Psychology (Division 24 of the American Psychological Association) and recipient of a Distinguished Lifetime Achievement Award from the Society.

Advances in Theoretical and Philosophical Psychology
Series Foreword
Brent D. Slife, Series Editor

Psychologists need to face the facts. Their commitment to empiricism for answering disciplinary questions does not prevent pivotal questions from arising that cannot be evaluated exclusively through empirical methods, hence the title of this series: *Advances in Theoretical and Philosophical Psychology*. For example, such moral questions as, "What is the nature of a good life?" are crucial to psychotherapists but are not answerable through empirical methods alone. And what of these methods? Many have worried that our current psychological means of investigation are not adequate for fully understanding the person (e.g., Gantt & Williams, 2018; Schiff, 2019). How do we address this concern through empirical methods without running headlong into the dilemma of methods investigating themselves? Such questions are in some sense philosophical, to be sure, but the discipline of psychology cannot advance even its own empirical agenda without addressing questions like these in defensible ways.

How then should the discipline of psychology deal with such distinctly theoretical and philosophical questions? We could leave the answers exclusively to professional philosophers, but this option would mean that the conceptual foundations of the discipline, including the conceptual framework of empiricism itself, are left to scholars who are *outside* the discipline. As undoubtedly helpful as philosophers are and will be, this situation would mean that the people doing the actual psychological work, psychologists themselves, are divorced from the people who formulate and re-formulate the conceptual foundations of that work. This division of labor would not seem to serve the long-term viability of the discipline.

Instead, the founders of psychology—scholars such as Wundt, Freud, and James—recognized the importance of psychologists in formulating their own foundations. These parents of psychology not only did their own theorizing, in cooperation with many other disciplines; they also realized the significance of psychologists continuously *re*-examining these theories and philosophies. This re-examination process allowed for the people most directly involved in and knowledgeable about the discipline to be the ones to decide *what* changes were needed, and *how* such changes would best be implemented. This book series is dedicated to that task, the examining and re-examining of psychology's foundations.

References

Gantt, E., & Williams, R. (2018). *On hijacking science: Exploring the nature and consequences of overreach in psychology*. London: Routledge.
Schiff, B. (2019). *Situating qualitative methods in psychological science*. London: Routledge.

A Philosophical Perspective on Folk Moral Objectivism
Thomas Pölzler

A Psychological Perspective on Folk Moral Objectivism
Jennifer Cole Wright

Suffering and Psychology
Frank C. Richardson

Suffering and Psychology

Frank C. Richardson

Routledge
Taylor & Francis Group

NEW YORK AND LONDON

First published 2023
by Routledge
605 Third Avenue, New York, NY 10158

and by Routledge
4 Park Square, Milton Park, Abingdon, Oxon, OX14 4RN

Routledge is an imprint of the Taylor & Francis Group, an informa business

ISBN: 978-1-138-30225-9 (hbk)
ISBN: 978-1-032-50264-9 (pbk)
ISBN: 978-0-203-73184-0 (ebk)

DOI: 10.4324/9780203731840

Typeset in Times New Roman
by Apex CoVantage, LLC

Dedicated to Carter and Tula Jo Richardson

Contents

Introduction

Modern psychology and psychotherapy are deeply motivated by a humane and compassionate desire to relieve human suffering of many kinds. However, they have concentrated almost exclusively on eradicating pain, suffering, and their causes in order to foster human freedom and fulfillment, at least as they delineate them. In doing so, psychology has uncritically perpetuated several questionable modern ideologies. These include a one-sided individualism and an overriding commitment to expanding instrumental control over events and oneself, ideals which foster a number of worthy ethical and practical outcomes but are distinctly limited and by themselves quite damaging or self-defeating in the long run. The purpose of this book is to explore the theoretical commitments and cultural values that have deterred the field of psychology from facing squarely and dealing credibly, as best they can, with inescapable human limitations and frailties, unavoidable suffering, pain, loss, heartbreak, and despair.

This book appears in a book series devoted to theoretical and philosophical psychology, a field in which I have worked with pleasure for several decades. I have often been struck how theoretical psychology, like the social sciences in general, tends to be fragmented into separate, largely unconnected areas of inquiry and lines of thought. Each may be somewhat interesting in its own right but never the twain shall meet, something for which we pay a significant intellectual price. Various schools of thought in theoretical psychology may address this problem and other shortcomings of mainstream psychology, such as phenomenology, critical theory, feminist perspectives, postmodern approaches, hermeneutic philosophy, virtue ethics, and a number of others. However, they too tend to run mainly on parallel tracks. Much would be gained if these diverse, rich approaches were brought into greater contact with one another and combined or cross-fertilized in some way. As a small step in that direction, I will try to incorporate elements from a number of these fertile schools of thought and explicitly include in my discussion a number of ideas from the works of several contemporary

DOI: 10.4324/9780203731840-1

theoretical psychologists that I find especially insightful and helpful, including "strong relationality" (Slife, 2004), "the priority of the other" (Freeman, 2014), "entrepreneurial selves" (Martin & McLellan, 2013), insights from Aristotle's ethics (Fowers, 2005), analysis of the phenomena of "empty" and "multiple" selves in modern times (Cushman, 1990; Cushman & Guilford, 1999), ethics and values in psychotherapy (Tjeltveit, 1999), and the philosophy of social science (Bishop, 2007).

Drawing on both secular and spiritual points of view, this book seeks to illuminate what Jonathan Sacks (2002) terms "transforming suffering," namely possibly finding meaning in suffering, or in a life that inescapably includes suffering, rather than mainly trying to eliminate it, anesthetize it, defy it, or treat it chiefly as a means to the end of other, ordinary kinds of fulfillment or well-being. Once one faces up to it, the realities of human suffering are mammoth and rather overwhelming. With trepidation, I hope to say some meaningful things about them that will interest both psychologists and some general readers. But my main purpose is to nudge the field of psychology, with careful arguments, toward giving greater attention to this dark and difficult dimension of the human struggle.

References

Bishop, R. (2007). *The philosophy of the social sciences: An introduction.* New York: Continuum.

Cushman, P. (1990). Why the self is empty. *American Psychologist, 45,* 599–611.

Cushman, P., & Guilford, P. (1999). From emptiness to multiplicity: The self at the year 2000. *Psychohistory Review, 27*(2), 15–31.

Fowers, B. (2005). *Virtue ethics and psychology: Pursuing excellence in ordinary practices.* Washington, DC: APA Press Books.

Freeman, M. (2014). *The priority of the other: Thinking and living beyond the self.* Oxford University Press.

Martin, J., & McLellan, A. (2013). *The education of selves: How psychology transformed students.* New York, NY: Oxford University Press. http://dx.doi.org/10.1093/acprof:oso/9780199913671.001.0001

Sacks, J. (2002). *The dignity of difference: How to avoid the clash of civilizations.* London: Continuum.

Slife, Brent. (2004). "Taking Practice Seriously: Toward a Relational Ontology." *Journal of Theoretical and Philosophical Psychology, 24,* 157–78.

Tjeltveit, A. (1999). *Ethics and values in psychotherapy.* London, UK: Routledge.

1 Stories of Suffering

As I talk to people in many different situations and walks of life, I discover that nearly everyone has a tale to tell about human suffering. It may concern their own loss, sorrow, or period of despair, the suffering of someone they know or were close to, or their own great pain at the suffering that someone they care about had to endure. Here is one of those stories.

Alex was a charmer and he led a charmed life. I knew him as an honors undergraduate student. We had a lot of common interests and he later became a good friend. Alex was nice looking, exuded an unforced pleasantness, and just naturally put nearly everyone at ease. One day another driver who felt Alex had cut him off in traffic honked at him loudly and sped past him gesticulating and cursing loudly. Alex calmly followed the driver for a couple of miles and pulled up behind him when he parked. He walked up to him as the driver was leaving his car. Alex spoke to the irritated and sullen fellow, apologized sincerely for any annoyance he had caused, and said he really did try to be as polite and understanding as he could on the road. There was enough antagonism in the world as it was, he smiled and said, no need to make it any worse. The other guy immediately relaxed and they chatted and laughed for a couple of minutes, shook hands, and went their separate ways. When he told me about it, I thought this was just typical Alex.

Alex worked very successfully in journalism for several years after college. He seemed to have a unique ability to get people to let down their guard and tell their stories. His colleagues and editors, all big-city liberals, were struck at how he could get information and rich commentary from conservative country folks, and how interesting, insightful, and humane he often showed them to be, in ways they would have missed entirely.

I lost track of Alex for a couple of years. One day we ran across one another on the street and went for coffee to catch up. I found out that six months earlier, returning home at dusk, in order to avoid a pedestrian suddenly crossing the street, he put his motorcycle down on the ground and sustained a serious head injury. He woke several days later in a rehab hospital

DOI: 10.4324/9780203731840-2

having lost all memory of the month before the accident. Two months later at home he suffered a brief relapse when he stopped taking his medications, feeling like he no longer needed them. It's just like me, he said. I always sensed something was wrong because I usually felt almost invulnerable. I've had such good luck with friends and girlfriends, and everywhere I go people offer me a job! But that's over now. Last week I visited my doc for a check-up at the hospital. A young man who looked a bit like me was pushed in a wheelchair by the open office door where he was paused for a moment. His face showed no expression, his head was lolled to the side and a little drool ran from the corner of his mouth, but our eyes locked for a few seconds. I was terrified. I felt like I had been flipped into another world. I asked the doc if someone like that would ever recover. Not likely, she replied (partly, he thought, to pressure him to take his meds regularly).

I don't think things will ever be the same, Alex said. "Welcome to the real world," he remarked. That fellow, whose name I don't even know, became a life companion, my secret brother, my wounded döppelganger. Maybe he will think of me as I will of him from time to time. Most of the joys and successes I have in life will be denied him as we both go on living. When something meaningful or loving does come his way, I feel like I should be there to hold his hand and tell him I haven't forgotten him. And I *can't* forget. How this will change how I feel or what I do in the future, I'm not sure. But everything seems different now.

Here is another tale of suffering, one in which waking up to the "real world" of suffering also plays a role. A few years ago, I attended a program at a local church on the struggles of veterans returning from the recent and current wars in Iraq and Afghanistan. One young vet who had written a moving little book on the topic related his experience of trying to commit suicide after his return, surviving, and now working to raise people's consciousness about the emotional and practical needs of so many of his comrades. Twice I expressed appreciation for his remarks but asked if these difficulties didn't say as much about our society's shallow and emotionally isolating way of life as about the struggles of vets. Many nodded their heads, but no one pursued the topic. Afterward, however, a couple approached me and expressed enthusiasm for that idea. I went out for coffee with them and heard their story.

Four or five years ago, Maryann and Sebastian's 14-year-old daughter Jackie developed stomach cancer, which was beginning to spread. Maryann took a leave from her job as a newspaper feature writer and traveled to stay with her daughter at a cancer treatment center in a large city in another part of the state. Physicians told her parents that a radiation and chemotherapy treatment regimen that would take six months or so had only about a 20 percent chance of saving Jackie's life. Maryann returned home each weekend.

The couple coped with the situation as best they could and clung to a bit of hope while trying to prepare for the worst. They grimly went about their business, comforting one another when waves of fear and grief would suddenly sweep over them.

In the end, to everyone's surprise and relief, Jackie recovered. She turned out to be one of the fortunate ones. She lost part of her stomach but seemed to be free of cancer. She finished high school and enrolled in college. Her parent's biggest concern now was encouraging and helping her to follow a healthy diet and never drink alcohol, college life notwithstanding, which could wreck havoc with a weakened digestive system. In one sense, things were almost back to normal. In another sense, Sebastian and Maryann found themselves living in a different world.

Only a few of their friends or colleagues at work were so distressed by their misfortune that they seemed to actively avoid Maryann and Sebastian. However, some of them still kept a bit of a distance. They would ask how things were going, sometimes, and express sympathy. But they appeared uncomfortable, seemed uncertain about what to say, and kept the conversation fairly short. Sebastian likened this situation to ones he had observed where someone was getting a divorce and many people around them seemed quite uncomfortable about it, as if they didn't want to be reminded of their own marital struggles, or somehow catch the divorce bug. Sebastian and Maryann were quite busy and not greatly bothered by these reactions; they had bigger fish to fry, but they took notice of them.

Maryann remarked, "The pain and dread we have been through has changed our outlook on a lot of things." When I asked just how, she replied with the account of a recent dream.

In the dream, before the cancer, we had been living on one side of a translucent screen or glass wall in a place where things seemed normal. We felt pretty much in control of our lives, and nothing terribly disturbing ever happened, at least not in close proximity to us. Out of the corner of my eye I could see faintly disturbing shadows on the other side of the screen, but I paid them little attention. Then, suddenly, everything switched and we found ourselves the other side. All around us we saw a hellish scene full of tragedy and pain. The people and their distress were actually familiar and commonplace, only now we could see them clearly, and couldn't look away. Brain-injured young men and women sitting in wheelchairs in a clinic, aware of their situation but hardly able to move or talk. Parents suffering unspeakable anguish at the death of a beloved child. Elderly people living by themselves, choking on their loneliness. Spouses being told their husband or wife had been killed in war and then struggling painfully with how to explain what has happened to their children.

Many other things, too, a panorama of them passed before us. Many thousands of young people in large cities and around the world with little education and no prospects for employment, sinking into despair, turning to violence, dying young. Mentally ill individuals of all sorts, frightened and often tormented, perhaps living their whole lives that way. There were disturbing scenes of war and bloodshed.

Maryann added,

I guess the message was that there may be lots of happy times and meaningful experiences to be had, if you're fortunate, but there is pain and suffering around every corner, and soon enough some of it will be yours. And, let's not forget, it is happening in a big way to many of our fellow human beings somewhere on the planet as we speak!

Sebastian added, "After Maryann told me about that dream, we started calling our life before Jackie's illness living in the 'pretend' world and life now as having to live in the 'real' world. The world seen without blinkers on."

There are or will be as many stories of dying and death as there are members of the human race. Here is one of them that came my way, which I asked Elizabeth to record for me.

When my sister Martha was diagnosed with brain cancer, it was a terrible blow for her and her family, her husband and two grown daughters. Our brother, our only other sibling, had died of a brain tumor a few years earlier, so we had a pretty good idea of what was coming. However, he passed away just a few months after his cancer was diagnosed, was never in physical pain, and seemed to face death with the same kind of "bonhomie" with which he had lived. In my sister's case, there were weeks, months, and then two years of coping with the disease and its ravages on body and mind. She went through two brain surgeries, chemotherapy, and "cyber knife" treatment. The first brain surgery to remove a large tumor at the back of her skull came on the Tuesday before her eldest daughter's wedding the following weekend. We were all amazed that she was able to attend the wedding. She looked beautiful, loved being there, danced with husband and friends, and talked to everyone. For me, it was a moment out of time. I was constantly aware that death was there with her. Every moment, every picture taken, every word exchanged seemed quietly charged and poignant.

Gradual physical and mental decline soon set in. I lived in a nearby city a little over an hour away but over the months I spent more and more time with my sister. Sometimes we talked a little, sometimes we just sat close together with me rubbing her back or holding her hand. In these moments, she made it clear how important I was to her, as she was to me. She suffered physically at times but worst was the terrible pain of knowing she was leaving her family, would not see her younger daughter get married, and would never meet her grandchildren. But she neither denied the reality of her situation or ever became bitter. Just one time she turned to me and said, "You know, our brother was the lucky one."

I remember a time toward the end when I went to visit. I opened the front door and my sister was standing there with a blank look on her face. I realized she was simply not there any longer. A neighbor happened to come by at that moment and I turned away and burst into tears. I felt like I couldn't bear it.

I stayed with my sister those last few weeks. We called in hospice and planned her funeral. Those were hard days for us all. At the same time there was a remarkable closeness between me and my sister. No barriers, no bounds, no pretending. There was a purity to our deep bond of love and affection different in part from anything we had experienced before. I came to see her more clearly than ever before. I saw through all the previous irritations with her to the beauty of her unique core of goodness—perhaps her soul. With a few little sighs and tiny hand squeezes, I think she had a sense that I was there looking our for her. Not that I could change anything or keep the sadness at bay, but that I was there.

As she seemed to hang on to life, I went home one day to sleep in my own bed. Twelve hours later, at four in the morning, I got a call saying that she had died. I returned at once. Her husband had notified the funeral home and they sent a van to pick up her body. Her husband and daughters could not watch as they wheeled the gurney into her bedroom, and then to the van. I'm nobody special, but I felt like her guardian angel, and felt that as my last act of love for my sister I needed to walk beside her those final steps.

I now see the complexity of suffering more clearly. Nothing can take away the sting of death. The pain, or some of it, remains. But there can be, it seems, a very deep connection, rich meaning, and, oddly, I say this with fear and trembling, a kind of peaceful joy in the suffering and the death of a loved one.

In each of these stories, individuals confronted suffering honestly and at least began to find a way to come to terms with it. However, we all know of circumstances of suffering that end badly, with resentment, cynicism, emptiness, or despair. Although it's never over until it's over, we go on living until we are no longer alive, and sometimes a significant shift in feeling or outlook takes place. Tolstoy's (2012) novella "The Death of Ivan Ilyich," which many feel is one of the greatest literary works of modern times, portrays such a shift on its protagonist's death bed in his last few hours.

Still, many times things end in pain and distress. This may happen with the death of a child. A couple in their 50s who are friends of a friend of mine recently lost their only son, suddenly, to an undiagnosed genetic heart defect. The young man was bright, loving, and engaged in a rich life of creative service endeavors. He had a fiancee and many friends and admirers. He and his parents were very close, talked all the time, and shared a fine life together. His mother said that driving home from the memorial service for her son on a Texas highway at 75 miles an hour it was all she could do to keep from opening the car door and throwing herself out. Her husband seemed able to distract himself somewhat from his pain only by tending to his wife and keeping a hand on her arm as he drove. The last I heard about them, a few weeks later, was that she recently had said: "There is nothing but darkness, dark days, ahead for me now."

There is no way to anticipate or predict how one is going to respond to suffering or loss. One does not choose meaning over despair, or the reverse, so much as find out what transpires as one goes through the experience. Like so much else in life, it is full of surprises and in the end simply a mystery. Nevertheless, the theologian Douglas John Hall (1986) sketches the issues involved in a general way that seems especially helpful. He writes that "suffering is real and the existential lot of humanity but may not be 'the last word about the human condition'" (p. 19). There is a "profound tension" between these two affirmations that is "hard enough to articulate" and "harder still to live within." In the realm of suffering, he suggests, "the human soul characteristically ranges" between two spiritual poles, namely "cynicism" and "credulity," both of which "are posited upon the false resolution of precisely this tension" (p. 20).

It's worth expanding a little on Hall's idea. Cynicism can take a trite and immature form. I remember hearing a number of people in business and professional circles, in the 1990s especially but also from time to time recently, in difficult or disappointing situations saying "Life's a bitch and then you die," as if that idea served to defensively ward off some degree of pain and despair. Cynicism may also take more refined forms in which one steels oneself against the pain in a brave, fatalistic manner. But as Rollo May said once, some people can courageously endure almost any kind of anguish. But then let them have a child, he commented, and all such defenses against vulnerability to fate are usually wiped away.

Credulity may involve simply obscuring or looking away from the hard facts of life. The old saw about young soldiers marching off to war filled with pity for the individual next to them who may be killed in battle illustrates this. In our kind of affluent society, many individuals confidently traipse on down the path to success and happiness largely oblivious to dreadful experiences they are likely to encounter in one form or another. Credulity may occur in simplistic religious formulations to the effect that tragic events are somehow "God's will." Or, more sophisticated theologizing or philosophizing may seek to lessen the sting by explaining how they really work for good in the long run, or that God cannot prevent much suffering so long as human beings have free will and may misuse it. But these formulations sound like rationalizations to many of us. They seem like attempts to dilute the hard reality of the suffering that is our "real and existential lot" (Hall, 1986) in ways that are less than convincing.

An admirable young woman I know and her husband had two healthy children. A third child was born in a severely weakened condition and shortly died. She said about this baby, rather touchingly, "That was going to be our last child, but God had other plans." I sensed that she may have a deeper and subtler sense of reverence in the face of the unknown than that remark of hers by itself conveys. However, although the reader might disagree, I would simply say that a God who allows some innocent babies to die and others to live according to a seemingly arbitrary "plan" that remains quite inscrutable to us is not a divinity I could believe in or find worthy of regard. Much popular Christianity, it seems to me, pays insufficient heed to Jesus' "Sermon on the Mount" where he says that we should love our enemies and pray for those who persecute us so that we may be children of the God who "makes his sun rise on the evil and on the good, and sends rain on the just and the unjust" (Matthew 5. 43–45, RSV). He finds in nature's indifference, of all things, to our conventional moralizing a figure of radical mercy and forgiveness, not evidence of a plan on the model of ordinary human concerns and aims that we have to find some tortured way to justify.

The main argument of this book is that a mature psychology needs to try to contribute to a wiser discussion of suffering, not predominantly offer a rather shallow discourse on stress, pain, and their remedy. Doing so would seem to involve beginning to explore the territory and dynamics of dealing with suffering between the poles of cynicism and credulity, and investigating what it might mean to live authentically in spite of the persistent draw of each of them.

References

Hall, D. (1986). *God & human suffering: An exercise in the theology of the cross.* Minneapolis: Augsburg.

Tolstoy, L. (2012). *The death of Ivan Ilyich.* (R. Peyear, & L. Volokhonsky, Trans.). New York: Vintage Books.

2   The Denial of Suffering in Psychology

It is hard to generalize about the vast sprawling enterprise of academic and professional psychology in our time, and one may be reluctant to criticize it when it plainly does some real good for some people. Nevertheless, although there are exceptions, it seems fair to say that most of the field seeks to describe or ameliorate a world seen with blinkers on, with much of the suffering, despair, and hopelessness screened out of the picture. Our theories and interpretations of research findings commonly speak about such things as "self-actualization," "effective behavior" or "self-efficacy," and "separation and individuation" as the natural course of human development as if these were obvious facts of life. In fact, they are anything but. They are ideals of the good and right life that blatantly, even if surreptitiously, proclaim the modern individualistic credo for living that many critics from Tocqueville in the 1830s down to the present argue advances a shallow and shaky program for living. While he did not provide us with a credible alternative, Michel Foucault (1987) seems to have put his finger on something important when he encourages us to aim for a more "mature adulthood" and desist from being either the perpetrators or victims of what he terms an intimidating "Enlightenment Blackmail," which might be freely translated as "Do you agree with my Enlightenment program of science, progress, and individualism, or are you an unenlightened dunce?"

This credo encourages us to overlook or downplay the great amount of heartbreak, suffering, physical and emotional pain, intense mourning, sense of meaninglessness, and dread that afflict nearly every person's life to some degree. These maladies tend to be acknowledged only as things to be eliminated or overcome by technology, social progress, or some kind of therapy. Many are, in fact, ineliminable, and at some level we know that, which can breed inner conflict and perhaps desperation. I recall giving a talk at a psychology convention and making a joke in the discussion period afterward about stories I had heard about medical staff at a cancer hospital in my hometown becoming irritated with terminally ill patients who seemed unable or unwilling to go through the

DOI: 10.4324/9780203731840-3

five stages of dying in the right order, ending, of course, in "acceptance." A distinguished-looking gentleman in his 50s in the audience remarked

> You laugh about it, but I have experienced something I think is similar. A year ago my wife of 30 years, with whom I was very happily married, died quite suddenly. It was not two or three months later that several friends of mine, one a psychologist, began pressuring me—it felt to me like guilt-tripping—to get out there and start "dating again." Instead of helping, it made me miserable. So far, I've declined the opportunity.

We all laughed, but many of us were also aghast.

Such denial of suffering easily becomes a major source of suffering in its own right. The great Buddhist teacher Thich Hnat Hanh passed away recently on January 22, 2022, at age 95. A moving obituary (Economist, 2022) notes that many distinctive sorts of modern suffering caught his eye, such as "the profit motive, the race to the top, the moment-by-moment distraction of devices, carelessness toward the planet." He told audiences at places like the Google campus "that voraciousness was just a way of papering over unhappiness. They did not need to be number one." Their marvelous inventions and creativity could focus mainly on "bringing healing; and they should practice 'aimlessness,' the art of stopping, looking into their lives and asking what they were running from."

In a psychology-saturated society like ours, it is difficult not to be a perpetrator or victim or both of this whitewashing the human condition. The theoretical psychologist Philip Cushman (2013), who has made an illustrious career of chiding psychology about its woeful blind spots, illustrates this problem. He recounts the psychoanalyst Maura Sheehy's (2011) story about a pregnant young woman who asked for an appointment because she was disturbed by "floaters," which are bits of protein floating in eye fluid that can be caused by pregnancy and can be annoying. The patient reports, "This is making me really anxious. I thought I should talk to someone so I can get over it and go on to have a great birth and a beautiful baby and be a happy mother" (p. 99). Sheehy comments about how this woman "'knows' she [is supposed to] . . . be serene, confident, happy, nondesiring, not anxious," but "if she continues down this road . . . unwanted emotions may surface" that will only increase the chances of the things she fears most occurring, such as a "difficult" birth or "an ugly, bad baby." These are things that are "not only possible" but "guaranteed" to happen, at times, to a number of people (p. 100).

Cushman (2013) notes that our children are vulnerable and our world is dangerous. "Becoming a parent requires a great deal of denial—perhaps even a delusion or two." He adds, "Birth visits upon our babies a myriad of hurts, unfairnesses, and tragedies" (p. 5). Besides the difficult and dark side of life in general, which middle-class Americans do not address well, mothers are faced with "structural absences and oppressions that leave new mothers with impossible expectations, little communal support, and intense fears of realistic danger" in a highly competitive, overworked, consumerist society (pp. 5–6). Nobody likes to think, he suggests, about how difficult parenting is and how painful it can be to watch a child get marked by the larger society in indelible and significant ways. "Floaters" abound. He adds, "And then of course there is always—always—the matter of death, ours and theirs, that we give them by bringing them into the world."

Cushman wonders how many of the emotional and interpersonal problems in today's world stem from our wider culture and politics' failure to address the difficult and dark side of things with something other than illusions, like the belief that "our babies will be safe . . . well adjusted . . . happy . . . and successful—contingent only on the mother's ability to perform properly" (p. 5). He suggests that much psychology only abets the problem by interpreting emotional pain as "solely intrapsychic, biochemical, or cognitive symptoms" rather than stemming from societal and existential conditions and offering primarily technical or narrowly instrumental approaches to treating it, such as medicalizing a mother's suffering as peripartum depression or PPD in the *DSM-V*—and then perhaps devising a manualized treatment for the problem.

The theoretical psychologist Ronald Miller (2004)—in a book with the title *Facing Human Suffering* that I wish I could have used for this volume— carefully documents some of the ways that contemporary psychiatry and psychology commonly obscure or deny the full experience and reality of human pain and suffering. Building on the analysis of the distinguished medical anthropologist Arthur Kleinman (1988), Miller points out that the

> amelioration of the suffering experienced by clients has been . . . reduced to . . . a concern with eliminating what are construed as the symptoms or manifestations of mental disorders, disabilities, diseases, and dysfunctions. The client's agony, misery, or sorrow is viewed as a mere epiphenomenon to be replaced by a description of a clinical syndrome . . . scientifically explained as the consequence of some technical design flaw in the person's nervous system, cognitive processes, or learning environment.
>
> (p. 39)

What gets lost in this translation, Miller (2004) argues, is "the meaning to the person of the injury, harm, or loss incurred," the "role of other individuals who contributed to or are affected by the injury, harm or loss," and "any sense of the moral consequences or ethical impact of the same" (p. 39). Even when aspects of the patient's malady are effectively treated, he contends, this kind of "dehumanization" can leave untouched or can even worsen an individual's suffering. We need to shift away from the "disease or biomedical model" and recognize "the importance of the everyday conception of suffering" (p. 41). Of course, Miller notes, this kind of objectification has given rise to holistic and alternative medical therapies, and to many humanistic protests against mechanistic and narrowly "instrumental" viewpoints in psychology (Richardson & Manglos, 2011). But he suggests these approaches face an uphill battle in an era of industrialized medicine and managed care.

However, in order to understand the roots of such undeniable reductionism and depersonalization and to effectively counter them, we need to dig deeper. As we discuss more fully in the next chapter, they are not simply the straightforward result of a runaway scientism or technicism. They have their roots in and are part and parcel of a particular "disguised ideology" concerning what life is all about that most people in modern society, in one form or another, are deeply attached (Bernstein, 1976; Richardson, Fowers, & Guignon, 1999). First of all, this is an *individualistic* outlook that relentlessly decontextualizes persons from history and culture and sets them, it is believed, on a path of their own free choosing, in order to protect them from dogmatism and moralism. But it does this at the price of drastically thinning out meaningful social ties or a sense of community that could afford individuals a sense of purpose, belonging, or direction beyond a fairly narrow kind of self-interest. One might say that it throws out the bathwater of rich human connectedness in order to get rid of the baby of arbitrary authority. Unfortunately, it leads, as has often been suggested, to psychological "emptiness," moral confusion, and a "culture of narcissism" (Cushman, 1990; Fromm, 1969; Lasch, 1978).

Moreover, this approach is strongly motivated to conceptualize human thought and action in strictly *instrumental* terms. It adopts a heavily anti-authoritarian stance that leads it to focus on more or less effective means to pre-given or goals or ends, the evaluation of which is left to purely personal inclination or choice. We are comfortable thinking in instrumental terms and resistant to questioning their adequacy to human life. Nowhere is this more the case than in most academic and professional psychology. We tend to see ourselves as in the business of finding more and more *effective* means to more and more *effective* personal living and social policies. After all, we might reply to any critic of this approach, do we want ourselves or others to be *in*effective in the business of living, do we? The only alternative to a relentless instrumental focus in our academic and professional endeavors seems to many to be dogmatism, mystification, idle whimsy, or, God forbid, ineffectiveness.

To overcome the depersonalization or dehumanization of illness and suffering Miller (2004) and Kleinman (1988) rightly complain about will require questioning our fervent dedication to a narrowly instrumental construal of our purposes and activities. But to do that, to somehow re-personalize our outlook on life and living, will mean more than simply ceasing treating human pain and suffering as mainly symptoms of a disorder that we hope to cure. The unanswered question is, what might we do instead? It will take something more that adopting a vaguely humanistic as opposed to mechanistic account of human behavior.[1] It will mean involve exposing ourselves to and contemplating the full range of human misery and suffering and considering afresh what in the world it might mean to come to terms with them. In doing so, quite apart from any religious or irreligious attitude we might entertain, we might appreciate St. Paul's observation of "the whole creation groaning for release." Of course, this means risking acute despair or a disturbing sense of meaninglessness, at least for a time, until, as sometimes happens, a transformed perspective on the human struggle and healing human ills emerges.

Note

1. I wish I had a dollar for every time I have heard presenters on programs discussing counseling or clinical psychology at APA meetings or elsewhere announce that they, perhaps for the first time they claim, have decisively overcome mechanistic or deterministic trends in therapy theory, rescued our freedom, and set us on a path to empowerment or self-actualization. They follow in the footsteps of many critics of Freud's mechanism and determinism, discussed later, who set out a cheerier vision of human prospects at the price of obscuring Freud's insights, however distored, into the dark and difficult aspects of the human condition.

References

Bernstein, R. J. (1976). *The restructuring of social and political theory.* Philadelphia: University of Pennsylvania Press.

Cushman, Philip. (1990). "Why the Self is Empty." *American Psychologist* 45: 599–611.

Cushman, P. (2013). Psychology's disavowed ethic: Psychologist as public intellectual. *Paper presented at the annual meeting of the American Psychological Association.* Honolulu, Hawaii.

Foucault, M. (1987). What is enlightenment? In P. Rabinow & W. Sullivan (Eds.), *Interpretive social science: A second look* (pp. 157–174). Berkeley, CA: University of California Press.

Fromm, Erich. (1969). *Escape From Freedom.* New York: Avon (Original publication 1941).

Kleinman, A. (1988). *The illness narratives: Suffering, healing and the human condition.* New York: Basic Books.

Lasch, Christopher. (1978). *The Culture of Narcissism.* New York: Norton.

Miller, R. (2004). *Facing human suffering: Psychology and psychotherapy as moral engagement.* Washington, DC: American Psychological Association.

Richardson, F., Fowers, B. & Guignon, C. (1999). *Re-Envisioning Psychology: Moral Dimensions of Theory and Practice.* San Francisco, CA: Jossey-Bass.

Richardson, Frank, and Nicolette Manglos. 2011. "Rethinking Instrumentalism." *Journal of Consciousness Studies* 17: 462–72.

Sheehy, M. (2011). Floaters. In M. Dimen (Ed.), With Culture In Mind (pp. 99–105). New York: Routledge.

3   Disguised Ideology

Michael Sandel (1996) depicts our way of life in American society as a "procedural republic" whose widely embraced public philosophy is one of "liberal individualism." One key element of that procedural republic is an "ideal of neutrality" according to which government should remain strictly neutral on the question of the good or decent life and insist only on tolerance, fair procedures, and respect for individual rights, respecting people's freedom to choose their own values. A second element of this way of life is the ideal of an "unencumbered self," the conception of a separate, choosing self that is subject to no obligations it has not itself authored or chosen, excepting only the obligation to respect the similar independence and rights of others.

If any social science, like psychology, were to breach this ideal of neutrality it would fall into severe disrepute. If it were to claim that its findings supported one or another conception of the good life, religious or nonreligious outlook, set of aesthetic standards, political party, or ethical system—other than the ideal of neutrality itself—it would lose its standing altogether. However, psychology garners the considerable prestige it does not because it is truly neutral in any thoroughgoing sense but because its disciplinary standards and taken-for-granted picture of a mature social actor mesh very well with the norms and practices of our procedural republic.[1]

In this chapter, I want to suggest that our way of life in the procedural republic goes about its business with blinders on concerning the dark and difficult side of human life that includes many kinds of human suffering and despair, which Maryann and Sebastian's experience related in Chapter 1 reveals. Moreover, the activities of the field of psychology, embedded in that way of life, tend to go about their business with similar blinders on. They obscure human suffering, or give only a truncated account of it, and as a result, overlook some of the more profound ways meaning is found in spite of it. First, in order to get a solid grip on these issues, I am afraid we need to dig into the conceptual weeds to a degree concerning the nature of the liberal individualism that Sandel (1996) identifies as our public philosophy

DOI: 10.4324/9780203731840-4

and that serves as the influential "disguised ideology" (Bernstein, 1973; Richardson, Fowers, & Guignon, 1999) of much modern psychology.

In many ways, the prestige and influence of contemporary social science, including the would-be "science" of psychology, are an enormous puzzle. The main goal of most social scientists over the last century or so has been to achieve a natural science of human behavior, on the model of what they take to be the very successful natural sciences. That would mean developing what has been called "empirical theory" (Bernstein, 1976, p. 14), namely universal, ahistorical, empirically confirmed laws or models of behavior that are logically derived from a few assumptions and definitions and permit precise prediction about events that are remote in space and time—possibly leading to instrumental power to manipulate social or psychological processes for worthy purposes and human betterment. I recall a few years ago discussing with a prominent social psychologist the social constructionist thinker Kenneth Gergen's (1982) claim that there simply are no universal laws of human behavior. "What would you do," I asked him, "if it turned out there were no such laws?" "Well," he replied, "I would certainly quit this field and maybe study instructional technology, which looks interesting to me, or possibly go into my family's construction business."

Indeed, without necessarily endorsing all of his particular brand of social constructionism, Gergen (1985) may be correct when he asserts that a "fundamental difference exists between the bulk of the phenomena of concern to the natural as opposed to the sociobehavioral scientist." In fact, he writes,

> there appears to be little justification for the immense effort devoted to the empirical substantiation of fundamental laws of human conduct. There would seem to be few patterns of human action, regardless of their durability to date, that are not subject to significant alteration.
>
> (p. 12)

Peter Winch (1958, 1977) clarifies why this is the case. He argues that human action is purposive, inherently social, "rule-governed" activity. In his view, explaining human action means giving an account of why people do the things they do—their motives, reasons, goals, and ideals—by reference to the intersubjective rules or standards that constitute their particular "form of life." So, to give a made-up example for illustrative purposes, imagine that correlational studies show that "self-efficacy" (Bandura, 1982) relates positively to a measure of personal well-being (which, by the way, would be a value-laden notion of good life prominent in a particular community or form of life). That correlation might disappear or no simply longer have any meaning if, for example, most in the community took the advice of the distinguished Buddhist writer Thich Nhat Hanh's (2021) advice and abandoned persistent individualistic striving, becoming practicing Buddhists who relinquished much in the way of attachment and found peace and well-being in becoming an "empty self." Thus, it should come as no surprise that so little in the way of genuine empirical theory, which the natural sciences have given us in abundance, has been achieved by social science inquiry (Bishop, 2007; Richardson et al., 1999; Root, 1993).

One wonders why so much social science, in the absence of desired results, has persisted in aiming at that goal. The philosopher David Hoy (1986) shrewdly observes that

> theory choice in the social sciences is . . . more relativistic than in the natural sciences, since the principles used to select social theories would be guided by a variety of values. Unlike a natural scientist's explanation, which relies on the pragmatic criterion of predictive success, a social scientist's evaluation of the data in terms of a commitment to a social theory would be more like taking a political stand.
>
> (p. 124)

Perhaps declaring theory and research results in much social inquiry is like performing rain dances in premodern communities. The purpose is not so hard-nosed pragmatic results, but a kind of propagation and meaningful celebration of a community's values and sense of what human life is all about.

What is the "disguised ideology," the ethical vision or political stand, that Hoy gestures at, which seems surreptitiously to animate much mainstream social science? We need to get clear as to what this reigning moral outlook is before we can identify the ways it deters us from fully facing human suffering. A key to the answer to this question, paradoxically, lies in the earnest intention of modern social science to be, as it is often put, "value free" or strictly ethically or politically neutral in all its methods and findings. To be sure, this ideal represents a latter day expression of the decent concern of many in the modern West to somehow avoid the violent clash of religious and political outlooks to which humans are exceedingly prone. Western culture has long been haunted by the mayhem of the European wars of religion following the Protestant Reformation, including the deadly Thirty Years' War (1618–1648) that killed about eight million people. The Peace of Westphalia (1648) lessened if it did not eliminate this kind of antagonism and conflict, setting the stage for a growing secularization, acceptance of religious pluralism, and attitude of tolerance in Western societies—with many unfortunate lapses into intolerance, hostility, and violence—down to the present day.

Christopher Lasch (1995) points out that the "drive to clean up politics" in the Progressive Era (roughly 1890 to 1920) in the United States "preached 'efficiency,'" 'good government,' 'bipartisanship,' and the 'scientific management'

of public affairs and declared war on 'bossism.'" They "launched compre-
hensive investigations of crime, vice, poverty, and other 'social problems."
Progressives "set out to create a welfare state as a way of competing with
the [political] machines" (p. 167). In this tradition, the notable author and
journalist Walter Lippmann (1922, 1925), an influential public intellectual
in his day, argued that a "complex industrial society required a government
carried on by officials who would necessarily be guided—since any form of
direct democracy was now impossible—either by public opinion or by expert
knowledge." However, public opinion "was unreliable because it could be
united only by an appeal to slogans and 'symbolic pictures.'" According to
Lasch, "Lipmann's distrust of public opinion rested on the epistemological
distinction between truth and mere opinion. Truth, as he conceived it, grew
out of disinterested scientific inquiry; everything else was ideology" (p. 169).

This homage to "disinterested scientific inquiry" should ring warning
bells for anyone who has studied or worked in the field of psychology. From
the first day in graduate training in academic or professional psychology,
one is encouraged to think of oneself as an "expert" whose theories, findings, and professional approaches are based on the best available "science"
and thus take convincing precedence over traditional ideals, given community standards, or the biased "ideologies" of politicians or preachers. Without that as a cornerstone of our professional identity, many of us, too, would
choose to go into some other line of work!

In Lasch's view, the progressive movement in many ways extended worthy secular, reformist trends, like a sensitivity to human rights and a hatred
of corruption and arbitrary authority; however, they might be rationalized.
No doubt, modern psychology has made similar, laudable contributions. But
Lasch argues that progressive thinkers to a troubling extent tended to throw
out the baby with the bath water. They tried to rise above the everyday, painful
human struggle for insight into what is really worth living for or what makes
for a good or decent society—a struggle in which everyone's opinion counts,
wisdom or insight can come from the most unlikely quarters, and dependence
on some of the wisdom of older traditions and sometimes even on the perspectives of very different "others," is essential. Without diminishing the value of
high intelligence and various kinds of expertise, empathy and humility play
a crucial role in the struggle, one full of surprises and unexpected learnings.
Borrowing a phrase from Aeschylus, we might say that it is "learning through
suffering." No one is exempt from the process, including would-be "experts,"
much as we might be tempted to defer to them. Navigating a social existence
guided by impersonal experts seems likely to be inauthentic and trivial.

It looks like the aspiration to disinterested scientific inquiry in psychology is motivated, too, by a concern to avoid entanglement in the frightening,
confusing, often seemingly irresolvable clash of moral visions and political

ideologies in a post-traditional, distressingly fragmented world, something that at times troubles everyone who is not just a fanatical partisan for one point of view or another. What a relief, supposedly, to escape that fray and yet be able to engage in the noble pursuit of a secure and practically useful knowledge of human life! But as Fowers (2005) points out, this claim to ethical neutrality is severely implausible. It demands a hard-won, disciplined, austere "detachment from the scientist's own cherished beliefs and outlook" that itself, ironically, represents a "central feature of a character ideal" (p. 20). Moreover, this ideal of detachment amounts to a confusing injunction that one ought to "value being value-free" (Slife, Smith, & Burchfield, 2003, p. 60), which opens the back door to the surreptitious embrace of a moral and/or political outlook that is at least questionable and that uncritically, even dogmatically, colors one's interpretation of data (or therapy patients).

This ideal hardly seems applicable to many phases of the search for understanding and wisdom that involve not detachment but in a sense the opposite, namely vulnerable, empathic, *engagement* with meaningful events and experiences, which can often involve suffering some amount of anxiety and emotional pain. We all know this from our common experience of trying to grow in understanding and wisdom in important human relationships with spouses, children, and friends. Such engagement takes place nowhere more than in facing and making sense of things when we suffer—heartbreak, disappointment, despair, loss, and all the rest. There is no way around except through. How could a valid kind of social and psychological inquiry operate exclusively on an entirely different plane of existence?

Liberal Individualism

The best single term I have found for the disguised ideology that underpins so much contemporary social inquiry is "liberal individualism." Liberal individualism is not some abstruse doctrine or rarified philosophy. It is commonplace, in the air we breathe. Cultural critics from Tocqueville (1969/1835) to the present day (e.g., Bellah, Madsen, Sullivan, Swindler, & Tipton, 1985; Cushman, 1990; MacIntyre, 1981; Root, 1993; and Taylor, 1989; and many others) have analyzed a one-sided individualism in our society culture that they feel promotes liberty and personal independence at the price of a great deal of debilitating alienation and emotional isolation. Quite often, you might notice, leading newspaper columnists and essays on current events make reference to an "individualism"—it has become almost a cliché—that makes it very difficult to show appreciation for a wider or common good (e.g., Brooks, 2018).

Charles Taylor (1975) traces the root of this problematic individualism. He discusses what he calls the modern problem of "situating freedom." Most modern conceptions of freedom typically portray it as something individuals "win through to by setting aside obstacles or breaking lose from external impediments, ties, or entanglements. To be free is to be untrammeled, to depend in one's action only on oneself" (pp. 155–156). Freedom understood as "self-dependence" contrasts with older definitions of it as "order or right relation" which is inseparable from carrying out one's obligations and finding one's fulfillment within some larger ethical or spiritual story.

In Taylor's view, modern conceptions of freedom tend to be "negative" in the sense that they define it mainly as "liberation," be it liberation from political oppression or from inner barriers to self-expression or self-creation. William Sullivan (1986) nicely summarizes some of the deleterious social consequences that flow from this stripped-down ideal of freedom. Sullivan contends that the "paradoxical effect of the growth of liberal capitalist society has been to undermine those social relations which have historically restrained and modified self-interested competition," thus tending to undermine even the honesty and trust necessary for the stable functioning of a market economy itself.

Most of modern psychology has been content to leave such social deficits to politicians to remedy and hand over any personal dysfunction or suffering incurred to medicine or some kind of psychological therapy. A partial exception is Erich Fromm (1941/65, 1947/75), a practicing psychoanalyst as well as leading social theorist, who insists on a broader view that connects the political and the personal. He felt that the personal disorientation this cultural configuration engenders was actually a major source of emotional problems in living in our current society. I want to add that it also depletes our resources for facing, making some sense of, and dealing the best we can with unavoidable human suffering.

Fromm (1947/75) argues that we have a well-developed sense of "freedom from" arbitrary authority and from dogmatic or irrational impediments to our freedom and to exercising greater control over nature and ourselves. However, we sorely lack a corresponding sense of "freedom to" or "freedom for" that would give some context, direction, and deeper purpose to our increased freedom and opportunity. The result, he thought, is that we tend to become interchangeable cogs in the social machinery, to become directionless and empty, to be led by the nose by whatever "sells" in the marketplace, including a widespread "personality market" in which we must try to revise even our personality make-up and basic motivations to accommodate the impulses or preferences of others. There is a lack of an inner moral compass to guide us in resisting whatever may be fashionable but still is shallow or corrupt. In a personality market we treat others and ourselves as depersonalized objects. Increasingly, one's "self-esteem depends on conditions beyond [one's] control."[2] The consequence is "shaky self-esteem," a constant "need of confirmation by others," and feelings of "helplessness, insecurity, and inferiority." Hungry for substance and for a more significant sense of purpose but unable to find them, in Fromm's view, we tend to sell out our freedom to fanaticism, the illusion of total fulfillment in romantic love, craving and seeking the approval of others at almost any cost, numerous other escapisms, or just going shopping.[3]

In his much-discussed recent book *Why Liberalism Failed*, Patrick Deneen (2018) traces this cultural outlook centered on individual autonomy back to the beginning of modern times. Deneen asks that we rethink in a fundamental way what we mean by "liberty." He argues that classical and Christian premodernity had long understood that the kind of liberty that alone forestalled tyranny was a "condition of self-rule" achieved through the cultivation of virtues or moral excellences such as "temperance, wisdom, moderation, and justice." It goes hand in glove with developing social norms and institutional forms that "check the power of leaders" and allow the "expression . . . (to varying degrees) . . . of popular opinion in political rule" (p. 22). Only such characters can resist the enticements of false prophets and take risks in standing up for one's best values. Thus, the personal and the political interpenetrate and support one another.[4]

Most importantly, such self-rule always involves a "limitation of desire" (Deneen, 2018, pp. 22–23). It involves self-discipline and giving precedence to the deeper satisfaction or sense of meaningfulness associated with the achievements of character over sheer quantities of momentary pleasure, worldly success, prestige, or possessions. An example might be the sense of happiness and pride and that parents enjoy when their child shows empathy for others or follows their conscience even though it risks disappointment or disapproval from others, compared with finding their primary satisfaction or reward in their child's competitive achievement in academics, athletics, or questing for greater prestige or popularity. Of course, the sense of meaningfulness that comes when one's child practices self-restraint or stands up for principle or weeps over the misfortune of another may not be immediately forthcoming. It may take time, courage, and patience to get to that point.

In conversations with students and others, I am struck by how many of them have an initial negative reaction to the idea of the "limitation of desire." They can readily come up with many fine examples of people being pressured to limit their desires or ambitions for dogmatic, moralistic, sexist, or neurotic reasons. But the idea of self-rule or true liberty that Deneen (2018) delineates is something they rarely talk about and even if they find it intriguing, they have trouble putting it into words in any acceptable form. Nevertheless, I find that they often have something sincere and sometimes quite profound to say about how just some such limitation of desire is a crucial aspect of the behavior they most admire in others or cherish in their most important relationships. Loyalty to friends in spite of the vicissitudes of popularity and the kind of sacrifices that parenthood commonly entails, from which they are aware they have benefited enormously, are frequently mentioned. This fits with the observation of Bellah et al. (1985)

that "individualism" is the "first language" of American moral and social discourse but that "second languages" of character and community often lurk, inarticulately, beneath the surface.

According to Deneen (2018), a "signal hallmark of modernity" was "the rejection of this long-standing view" of self-rule in personal and political realms. The effort to foster virtue was seen as "both paternalistic and ineffectual," as prone to moralistic abuse and the arbitrary exercise of authority, and as powerless to contend with human selfishness, greed, and pride (as Machiavelli forcefully argued). The novel solution proposed was to base politics "upon the reliability of 'the low' rather than aspiration to 'the high'" (p. 24). In this approach, "liberty" is significantly redefined as the "liberation of humans from established authority, emancipation from arbitrary culture and tradition, and the expansion of human power and domination over nature" (p. 27). A much more effective curb on incurably base or self-interested human proclivities can be provided by strictly external constraints, by "the legal prohibitions and sanctions of a centralized political state" (p. 26). Moreover, such laws and sanctions can channel such tendencies in the service of greater productivity and accomplishment. Who among us hasn't heard someone rationalize strictly self-interested or greedy behavior as something that is OK because contributes to the greater economic or even social good. The popular 1987 movie "Wall Street," containing the famous line "Greed, for want of a better word, is good," managed to both celebrate and mock such an attitude.

Deneen agrees that what he terms this new "liberal voluntarist" conception of human nature and agency has contributed to a large expansion of human rights, human dignity, and the elimination of many superstitious, arbitrary, irrational limits on human powers and creativity, work that remains unfinished today. But it never has explained how profoundly self-interested human persons can be motivated to craft law and policy that will effectively contain strong drives for power and possessions. This approach somehow manages, paradoxically, to be brutally realistic bordering on cynical about human nature and at the same time wildly optimistic, almost utopian, about its material and moral prospects—a confusing and uncomfortable tension I suspect most of us find we have to live with. What transpires is that those who can are likely to use every political and legal means available to enhance and preserve their own and their children's privileged economic and social ascendency. Brill (2018) and Stewart (2018) have documented how just this phenomenon has mushroomed recently with a "new aristocracy" in American society, about 10 percent of the population that is economically secure and leads a relatively secure and comfortable good life. The rest struggle economically, are no longer upwardly mobile, and may not be able to afford a vacation, an adequate retirement, or to send their children to college. Over time, this situation has "corrosive social and civic effects." It "[u]ndermines any appeal to common goods" and "induces a zero-sum mentality" that infects many different spheres of life and thought (Deneen, 2018, p. 29).

Deneen (2018) mentions briefly that the modern liberal outlook (again, both conventionally left-leaning and right-leaning) typically emphasizes the inherent "dignity" as well as the rights of would-be autonomous individuals. Such dignity is at least a residue, or perhaps a stripped-down version, of traditional views of persons gaining a sense of dignity and worth as a small part of some wider meaningful cosmic order, for example as being "made in the image of God" in the biblical account or, in Buddhism, finding peace in becoming an "empty self."

Some see such traditional views as reflecting an indispensable wisdom while others see them as outmoded and unnecessary. I would stress that for everyone except the most bitterly cynical, *some* sense of human dignity forms an essential part of the modern liberal moral outlook, however difficult it may be to explain or justify in the terms of that outlook alone.

The psychiatrist and noted author Robert Coles (1987), when he toured the USA, found that, no matter where he went, people were quite ready to speak in a psychologically charged vocabulary about their "problems" and "issues." "The hallmark of our time," he writes, is "lots of psychological chatter, lots of self-consciousness, lots of 'interpretation'" (p. 189). Psychology here means "a concentration, persistent, if not feverish, upon one's thoughts, feelings, wishes, worries—bordering on, if not embracing, solipsism: the self as the only or main form of (existential) reality." Robert Bellah and his colleagues (Bellah et al., 1985, p. 143) use the term "ontological individualism" to describe this widespread modern notion that the basic unit of human reality is the individual person, who is assumed to exist and have determinate characteristics prior to and independent of his or her social existence. Social systems, in this view, must be understood as artificial aggregates of individuals which are set up to satisfy the needs of those individuals. Ontological individualism serves as one of the key elements of a modern way of life with its stress on personal autonomy and individual self-realization, its sharp distinction between public and private realms, and its tendency to privilege or idealize relatively "thin" or merely contractual ties between individuals who cooperate or compete for ultimately individual ends.

However, it must be emphasized that there is usually more to the modern liberal outlook than unalloyed ontological individualism. This kind of individualism typically counterbalances a heavy stress on self-interest and personal self-realization with a serious emphasis on regarding human agents as possessing human or natural rights and imbued with dignity and inherent worth. Sullivan (1986) helpfully suggests we picture this view as an ellipse with two foci. One focus is a principle of profound self-interest. The other is an ideal of sacrosanct human rights and dignity. Together they comprise the dominant secular faith of many modern societies.[5]

First formulated by the philosopher Kant, this approach centers on *formal* principles of *procedural* justice or fairness (Neal, 1990; Rawls, 1971). Such principles "constitute a fair framework within which individuals and groups can choose their own values and ends, consistent with a similar liberty for others" (Sandel, 1996, p. 11). The purpose of this scheme is to avoid designating any particular ends in living or ways of life as superior while still assuring respect for individuals and their choices. In the mental health field, we adopt this approach by talking about more or less "effective" therapeutic means to reaching ends that we often label "health" or "well-being," as if these ends were purely given by nature or chosen by clients without any outside influence. We maintain *both* our neutrality about others' choices *and* our dedication to their welfare in a way that obscures how much "health" is always, in part, defined by cultural and moral norms, and how much we influence clients in adopting or reworking the meanings they live by (Christopher, 1999; Fancher, 1995; Richardson et al., 1999; Tjeltveit, 1999). These meanings are assumed to exist inside the client, rather than being something shaped in interaction with others in the social world. Therapists who think in these terms can blithely assume that they are merely facilitating a natural developmental process that is unaffected by their personal influence. However, as the psychoanalyst and author Irwin Hoffman (1996) observes, this is simply not the case:

> When we interpret the transference, we like to think that we are merely bringing to the surface what is already "there," rather than that we are cultivating something in the patient and in the relationship that might not have developed in the same way otherwise . . . our hands are not clean.
> (p. 109)[6]

So, liberal individualism represents a sincere effort to affirm freedom without dissolving responsibility. It seeks to eliminate dogmatism without abandoning our moral duties to others. Nevertheless, this approach is fatally one-sided. It is embroiled in the paradox of advocating a thoroughgoing *neutrality* toward all values as a way of *promoting* particular basic values of liberty, tolerance, and human rights. Justice is strictly procedural, which means that the focus is on *formal* rules or codes that we hope will protect our rights and prerogatives while ensuring that no one can define the good life for anyone else. However, if we cannot reason together meaningfully about the worth of ends, we also cannot defend liberal individualism's *own* vision of a way of life characterized by dignity and respect (Sullivan, 1986, p. 39). A serious commitment to human rights and dignity clearly sketches out a way of life that is taken to be morally superior or *good in itself*. But what is to prevent a principled neutrality toward all notions of the good life from extending to those basic values of liberty and human dignity as well, undermining their credibility, and stripping them of any possibility of rational defense (Kolakowski, 1986; Sarason, 1986)? A slide toward moral relativism and social fragmentation seems inevitable.

On a practical level, liberal individualism's insistent characterization of human action and motivation as exclusively self-interested seems likely to be a self-fulfilling prophecy. The direct pursuit of security and happiness seems progressively to dissolve the capacity to respect and cherish others (Bell, 1978, p. xv ff.). If so, this kind of individualism fails to provide us with a credible ethical outlook for our confusing modern times. Jerome Frank (1978, pp. 6–7), the distinguished psychologist and historian and critic of modern psychotherapy, argues that whatever may be learned from countervailing traditional values such as "the redemptive power of suffering" or "self-restraint and moderation" gets lost in this modern outlook. Also, it has the effect over time of undermining even the highest modern ideals of freedom and justice that are supposed to temper unbridled self-interest.

The "Critique of Instrumental Reason"

The noted legal scholar and social theorist Philip Selznick (1998, pp. 6 ff.) astutely summarizes both the positive and the self-undermining aspects of the modern liberal outlook. He writes that the "transition from sacred to secular modes of thought enhances morality in that it tends to reduce narrow-mindedness and bigotry." Still, this modern outlook brings benefits of greater individual freedom, increased equality of opportunity, efficiency, and accountability, and the rule of law only at the price of "cultural attenuation" and "some loosening of social bonds." Thus, there has been a "movement away from densely textured structures of meaning," like a shared mythology, time-honored customs, or fundamental character ideals, even if they must be often revised, to "more abstract forms of expression and relatedness," like being a private individual in a liberal democracy or market economy. This movement "may contribute to civilization—to technical excellence and an impersonal morality—but not to the mainsprings of culture and identity." The price to be paid for "cultural attenuation" becomes clearer with the passage of time. As Philip Selznick puts it, "modernity, especially in its early stages, is marked by an enlargement of individual autonomy, competence, and self-assertion. In time, however, a strong, resourceful self confronts a weakened cultural context; still later, selfhood itself becomes problematic."

I suggest that liberal individualism unravels because of the shortcomings of two main cultural ideals. One is the liberal voluntarist depiction of the human agent or self (Deneen, 2018). The second is "instrumentalism" (Richardson & Manglos, 2012) or a heavily one-sided emphasis on "instrumental rationality" (Habermas, 1973; Horkheimer, 1974; Horkheimer 1974). Instrumentalism is mentioned less often than individualism as a source of disarray by cultural critics and critical psychologists. But the two go hand in hand and the latter, in my view, is of immense significance.

Charles Taylor (1995, p. 7) concisely captures their complementarity. First and foremost, individualism decontextualizes the knowing subject from the ongoing flow of practical life and human relationships. Taylor points out that this view fits well with the widespread modern picture of the self as disengaged, disembodied, and atomistic or "punctual." This self is "distinguished . . . from [the] natural and social worlds, so that [its] identity is no longer to be defined in terms of what lies outside . . . in these worlds" and when mature, is ready to freely and rationally treat both itself and the outside world instrumentally, in order to advance desired individual or social ends. Taylor argues that the modern notion of a "punctual self" confronting a natural and social world to which it has no essential ties is as much a *moral* as a scientific ideal. It "connects with . . . central moral and spiritual ideas of the modern age," especially the modern ideal of "freedom as self-autonomy . . . to be self-responsible, to rely on your own judgment, to find your purpose in yourself" (p. 7).

The critical theory of the famous Frankfurt school (Held, 1980) and Jürgen Habermas (1973, 1991; McCarthy, 1978) cut to the quick of the problem of our overweening celebration of instrumental reason. Indeed, I would suggest that many of the shortcomings of contemporary social science could well be addressed by "going back to the future" through their reflections. Unfortunately, they have received scant attention in the field of psychology.

The cornerstone of this kind of critical theory is its "critique of instrumental reason." Habermas (1973) sums up this critique by arguing that modern society to a great extent is built upon a harmful confusion of *praxis* with *techne*, Greek words meaning roughly culturally meaningful activities and narrower technical capacity. This kind of society tends to collapse the cultural and moral dimensions of life into merely technical and instrumental considerations. As a result, "the relationship of theory to praxis can now only assert itself as the purposive-rational application of techniques assured by empirical science." Unfortunately, such applications "produce technical recommendations, but they furnish no answer to practical [or moral] questions" (Habermas, 1973, p. 254). Many spheres of life have become dominated by a calculating and instrumental viewpoint that discerns means-ends relationships, performs cost-benefit analyses, and seeks to maximize our control or mastery over events. As noted earlier, Fromm (1947/75) points out this may increase our instrumental prowess in some areas but undermines our ability to evaluate the worth of ends on any basis other than the sheer fact that they are preferred or desired.

In an especially clear and incisive Frankfurt School treatise *The Eclipse of Reason*, Max Horkheimer (1947/2013) argues the modern outlook which venerates instrumental reason actually turns into its opposite or an "eclipse of reason." Scientific "neutrality" that regards all values as merely subjective undermines our ability to reason together about the inherent quality of our way of life and about what ends in living we might best seek. As the means of control and influence grow, social life becomes more extensively organized, bureaucratized, and complicated, but we lose the ability to set priorities and impose needed limits. In this way, critical theory sheds light on our tendency to despoil the environment, our fascination with power and control to the neglect of other important values, and our stressful, overextended lifestyles.

It cannot be emphasized how much the field of psychology incorporates and perpetuates this "eclipse of reason." As Fowers (2005, p. 102) points out, "The quest for effectiveness is a ubiquitous and driving aim in psychology." This is "amply evident in the recurrent vocabulary of our field, with its emphasis on skills, techniques, instruments, mechanisms, effects, efficacy, results, and outcomes." All this emphasis on identifying strategies and methods producing desired results "serves the societal and professional project of maximizing control and mastery," at the expense of any other goals or ways of appreciating or enjoying our lives.

Rarely but occasionally someone in the field of psychology gains insight into this problem. For example, a number of years ago the distinguished historian and critic of modern psychotherapy Jerome Frank (1978, pp. 6–7) argued that as "institutions of American society, all psychotherapies . . . share a value system that accords primacy to individual self-fulfillment," including "maximum self-awareness, unlimited access to one's own feelings, increased autonomy and creativity." The individual is seen as "the center of his moral universe, and concern for others is believed to follow from his own self-realization." In Frank's view, although these values are admirable in many ways, modern therapy is still morally ambiguous. He notes that the implicit value system of modern psychotherapy "can easily become a source of misery in itself" because of its unrealistic expectations for personal happiness. He expresses regret that the literature of psychotherapy gives little attention to such traditional, possibly worthwhile values or virtues as "the redemptive power of suffering, acceptance of one's lot in life, adherence to tradition, self-restraint and moderation" (pp. 6–7).[7]

The critical theorists distinguished between what they termed "traditional" theory that was modeled on the natural sciences, including Marxism, which they felt retained key elements of a positivistic or scientific materialist viewpoint, and "critical" theory that sought to liberate modern souls from the dominance of instrumental reason that in many ways enslaved them (Horkheimer, 1947/2013). They hoped to contribute to the transformation of modern society as a whole. There isn't the space here to delve into the matter further, but it is widely acknowledged that the Frankfurt School and their followers never came up with a genuine or convincing alternative to traditional theory (Held, 1980; Moon, 1983; Richardson & Fowers, 1998). This underscores the fact that credible alternatives to individualism and instrumentalism—especially ones that do not threaten cherished modern freedoms or put an arbitrary damper on our technological prowess, however much we may regret their excesses—have proved very hard to imagine.

Liberal Individualism and Suffering

Liberal individualism is our dominant social credo. This does not mean that other kinds of moral or spiritual values do not have some sway in our lives. They often do. But they are usually on the defensive. They have difficulty explaining and justifying themselves and we have difficulty finding time for their cultivation or pursuit in a world where our common sense, advertising, much popular entertainment, and the social sciences all tell us that life is primarily a business of pursuing autonomy and effectiveness. It is fascinating how many movies and television dramas retell the story of someone breaking free from a suffocating family or community, pointless moralisms or conventions, emotional struggles, addictions, or just the well-meaning but muddled influence of others in order to finally "find themselves" or "discover their own path." The goal for them, stated explicitly or clearly implied, seems indeed to be becoming an "unencumbered self" (Sandel, 1996), a separate, choosing self largely subject only to obligations it has itself authored or chosen. What happens when they find this path, however, is rarely explored. The stories end in the middle or usually don't go on long enough for us to learn how, after being "liberated" or "empowered," they might struggle with Fromm's problem of our lacking a compelling "freedom for." To put it another way, they fail to show how inadequate, by themselves, the ideals of liberation and empowerment are to deal with the kind of moral confusion, emptiness, or existential deadness that are quite familiar today.

These ideals are inadequate because of a glaring blind spot in the liberal individualist outlook. This blind spot concerns the many aspects of human life that simply are entirely beyond our control. Some insightful analyses by historians of ideas and social theorists of the concept of "stress" in current social discourse neatly expose the problem (including Becker, 2013; Cooper & Dewe, 2004; Hutmacher, 2019; Kugelmann, 1992; Pollock, 1988; Rosa, 2010, 2013). Being "stressed out" has become what Hacking (2007) calls a particular, culturally shaped "way to be a person, to experience oneself, to live In society" (p. 299). Hutmacher (2019) comments, "Besides being a theoretical construct that is used extensively in research, the concept of stress has permeated into our daily lives."[8]

People have always had to deal with many different kinds of difficulties and hardships on a regular basis. Interestingly, however, it appears that before the Second World War, "no one spoke of stress; after it, increasingly, everyone did" (Kugelmann, 1992, p. 54). In his perceptive analysis of this development, Hutmacher (2019, p. 182) writes that "stress can be viewed as a fuzzy and versatile concept expressing the vague notion that 'things are getting too much and out of balance.'" He suggests that conceiving of oneself as being stressed announces that one is participating fully in our pell-mell and harried way of life while hoping and trying to cope with its relentless pressures. Thus, being stressed out can be seen as a badge of honor. It means that one is a player, aims at success rather than accepts failure, or has the drive or will power to persevere whatever the obstacles one faces. As a result, there has cropped up a varied armada of therapeutic and self-help coping strategies, including yoga classes, meditation, mindfulness-based stress reduction, coaching, cultivating spirituality, and many others, to aid in keeping one's balance while still rushing ahead in much of life. They wouldn't exist if they were not sometimes beneficial. But the overall project of stressful but rewarding living easily miscarries.

Liberal individualism precariously holds onto an ethical principle of respecting the rights and dignity of others. But its main ideal concerns advancing personal autonomy and maximizing instrumental control over events and oneself. This approach engenders a way of life of "acceleration" (Rosa, 2013) and "flexibilization" (Sennett, 1998, 2006). There develops an ongoing "acceleration cycle" (Rosa, 2010, p. 16) of rapid technological development, accelerating social change, and a speeded-up pace of life. Ironically, people long for technological innovations that they hope will save them time and energy but only lead to escalating social change and a quickened pace of life! Rosa (2010) suggests that in increasingly secular modern societies, people think much less about the afterlife, which many simply no longer believe in, or their standing with God or eternity. Rather, "the richness, fullness, or quality of a life . . . can be measured from the sum and the depth of experiences made in the course of a lifetime." (Of course, none of this eliminates threats of meaninglessness or the sting of death.) However, the number of options grows faster than the available time or means to take advantage of them. One can't win for losing. Any sense of mounting limitations or lost opportunities is likely to be intensified by renewed efforts to expand the quality of one's life in this sense.

This dynamic may be reflected in a lead article in The Washington Post (4/8/19) entitled "Burnout Nation: Chronic Stress is Everywhere, and It's Taking It's Toll." Shortly after that article appears another entitled: "There a Serious Problem Plaguing Some Older People: Loneliness." This gives the appearance that for many people there are two possibilities, namely become seriously stressed out or suffer acute loneliness when one no longer competes in the game of life.

The sociologist and social theorist Richard Sennett (1998, 2006) perceptively describes how flexibilization contributes to this problem. (Although, like many otherwise astute social critics, he has little to say about credible alternatives.) Classical capitalism commonly compelled industry workers to repeatedly perform the same movements over and again without any overview of the production process as a whole. But, he notes, the culture of a new so-called "Post-Taylorist" capitalism requires a different kind of person and worker who "can prosper in unstable, fragmentary conditions" (2006, p. 3). She or he must cope with uncertainty and unpredictability, be ready to learn new skills and adapt to new circumstances, accept that everything is transient and everyone can be easily replaced, and accept that they do not have a fixed place in the world. As Sennett (2006, p. 5) puts it simply: "Most people are not like this." Many, at least, desire much more than is possible in such a world in the way of security, predictability, and peace of mind.

Whether they embrace the modern acceleration cycle or try to escape it, many people tend to be caught in a trap that Hutmacher (2019) terms an ultimately fruitless effort to "control the uncontrollable." One might think, as distress grows with no end in sight, that more of us would reflect on how to make serious revisions in this way of life. However, as Hutmacher points out, we largely take for granted deep-seated assumptions about our fundamental identity as modern persons that make it almost impossible to rethink such striving.

For example, a key facet of our modern identity according to Taylor (1989, pp. 211 ff.) is a particular kind of "affirmation of ordinary life." In traditional societies and moral philosophies like Aristotle's ethics, the activities of ordinary life, including such things as marriage and family life, crafts, and economic activity serve primarily as a context or infrastructure for the pursuit of "higher" goods or excellences. Post-Reformation views, however, regard living well as less a matter of participating in some higher or nobler activity, such as contemplation or monastic life and more a question of just *how* this ordinary life itself is lived. Society increasingly secularizes under the pressure of a profound anti-authoritarian impulse, revulsion at religious dogmatism and violence, and growing delight in the achievements of natural science and its remarkable technological applications. Emphasis on living a godly, reverent life has been gradually transmuted into a concern to foster individual contentment, fulfillment, or well-being.

The kind of liberal individualism that results from this shift contains a meaningful residue of traditional values, such as regarding individuals as "made in the image of God," in the form of respect for the dignity, equal worth, and natural or basic human rights of every person. Commentators and politicians often term these ideals "sacred." Moreover, most of us would welcome an outlook on life that fully appreciates, when they are available, "ordinary life" experiences of friendship, simple comforts, sexual love, athletic activity, the joys of child-raising, the satisfaction of carrying out everyday responsibilities in work and family life, and so forth. An unqualified affirmation of such human goods is surely one of the blessings of modern culture.

However, there is a fly in this ointment. The ideal of the affirmation of ordinary life declares that such experiences, accessible to everyone, are "good" or "meaningful" in a strong sense that has nothing to do with any elite, inherently superior, or religiously austere status. But philosophically speaking, it is difficult, in the absence of any higher tier or vital dimension of ethical or spiritual life, to explain just what that goodness or meaningfulness is or just *why* such ordinary life is good, decent, or worthwhile. Does this situation mean then, as a philosopher once put it, that there simply is no difference between poetry and porridge? How exactly are these meanings of ordinary life indistinguishable from mere brute satisfactions or idle titillations?

In a practical sense, as well, many cultural critics worry about this matter. The distinguished Czech playwright and widely admired public intellectual Václav Havel (1995) notes that many outside the modern West esteem and aspire to its "ideas of democracy, human rights, the civil society, and the free market." But they hesitate when they see a "demoralizing and destructive spirit" also emerging in the West. They worry that the inevitable by-product of liberal democracy is

> moral relativism, materialism, the denial of any kind of spirituality . . . a profound crisis of authority . . . a frenzied consumerism, a lack of solidarity . . . [and] an expansionist mentality that holds in contempt everything that in any way resists the dreary standardization and rationalism of technical civilization.

This ambiguity concerning liberal democracy may reflect the ethical insufficiency and progressive unraveling of liberal individualism, our main cultural credo. This outlook asserts that every person has equal worth and essential human rights. Respect for those rights is a morally serious ideal. However, a large part of its human value consists in granting individuals the opportunity to participate, strive, and compete for possessions, opportunities, security, and status. Individuals who are inclined toward more modest or contemplative ways of living may be able to attain them to some degree. But they usually have to join in the competitive fray and compromise those more contemplative or pacific aims in order to survive. The drive for security and advantage often does painful battle in their minds and hearts with more peaceful aspirations. So whether one embraces ceaseless instrumental striving or seeks to escape it, the result is often grave disappointment and distress.

A consequence of our relentless efforts to control the uncontrollable, rooted in a morally ambiguous "affirmation of ordinary life," is great difficulty facing and somehow coming to terms with ubiquitous human suffering. Moreover, it generates additional kinds of suffering of its own. In a powerful essay entitled "Liberalism is Loneliness," Christine Embra (2018) illuminates the more personal side of this way of being. She summarizes some of Deneen's (2018) ideas, she writes that fundamentally "liberalism defines humans as autonomous and rights-bearing individuals who should be freed up as much as possible to pursue their own preferences, goals and dreams." Classical liberalism "celebrated the free market, which facilitated the radical expansion of choice." Left-leaning liberalism "celebrated the free market, which facilitated the radical expansion of choice." But both approaches "basically converge into the same thing: a headlong and depersonalized pursuit of individual freedom and security that demands no concern for the wants and needs of others, or for society as a whole." Quoting Deneen (2018) she notes that liberalism progresses by ever more efficiently liberating each individual from "particular places, relationships, memberships, and even identities—unless they have been chosen, are worn lightly, and can be revised or abandoned at will." In the process, it has scoured anything that could hold stable meaning and connection from our modern landscape

As a result Embra (2018) writes, on a personal level "we've all been left terribly alone. Liberalism is loneliness. The state isn't our sibling; the market won't be our mate. The state isn't our sibling; the market won't be our mate." The market may offer you the chance to purchase more in the way of satisfaction and security to fill the void of meaning, the left may provide you with more regulations to protect you in your search for them. But

> the more either the right or left's solutions attempt to fill in the gaps . . . the more obvious it becomes that the entire concept is flawed. The institution of liberalism[9] is caving in on itself, and we each individually *feel the crush.*

Our society's paramount concern and commitment to expand control over events and ourselves to meet our needs and satisfy our preferences, and to protect individual rights to participate in and benefit from that kind of progress, makes it almost impossible to face indelible human limits and ubiquitous human suffering. They have little meaning except as something to eliminate, avoid, or heal. Of course, increasing the safety and security of persons, advancing human rights, and healing bodily and psychological ills are generally admirable, even noble pursuits. But unless they take place as part of a way of life that includes a recognition of fundamental human limitations, including unavoidable suffering and death, and seeks some sort of meaning that may not be destroyed by them, they lose much of their dignity and depth.

It is for this reason, in a book entitled *Truthfulness and Tragedy*, that the prominent moral theologian Stanley Hauerwas (1977) includes a chapter entitled "Medicine as a Tragic Profession." In modern society, Hauerwas suggests. we "tell ourselves false stories about the nature and power of medicine" (p. 202). Medicine

> has been sustained by a story that has as its purpose to eradicate or at least to mitigate as completely as possible the fact of chance from our lives. Chance is fate and fate is death. The goal of autonomy and freedom makes us enemies of chance.

Hauerwas notes that in this respect, "medicine is in harmony with the major ethical positions of our day." For modern persons, typically, even for the "modern ethicist," chance or fate represents an "irrational surd." We all know that "morality must have to do only with those matters that we can do something about. Control, not chance, is the hallmark of the moral man" (p. 200).

This was not always the case. Hauerwas (1977, p. 204) reminds us that "for the Greeks it was chance or fate that they took to be central to the moral life. It was the man who knew how to respond to his fate appropriately who was the truly moral man." In the Christian tradition, he notes, the category of fate has a place, but it was "transformed by the use of the language of gift, that is as grace." Only the person who "knows how to accept a gift" can be on the road to moral depth and maturity because she "had the moral basis to understand" that she "was not under the power of indifferent fate but rather subject to Providence." The ability to accept a gift contrasts sharply with a determination to be in control. All the world's great spiritual traditions make appreciation and participation in some wider meaningfulness or higher order of being the key to living a good or full life. Later I will make mention of some secular as well as spiritual points of view centering on compassion and service to others that also attempt to provide a serious alternative to modern individualism and instrumentalism and open the door to a more honest approach to suffering. First, however, it may be helpful to put these struggles with fate, chance, and suffering in at least a sketch of a longer historical perspective.

Notes

1. Not unlike the Moscow Trials of the 1930s, appropriately horrific to us, fit well in the context of an authoritarian Marxist-Leninist people's democracy.
2. A few years later, in a compact and elegant manner, Hans-Georg Gadamer (1981, pp. 73–74) made a similar point. He wrote:

   > The individual in society who feels dependent and helpless in the face of its technically mediated life forms becomes incapable of establishing an identity . . . In a technological civilization . . . in the long run the adaptive power of the individual is rewarded more than his creative power. Put in terms of a slogan, the society of experts is simultaneously a society of functionaries . . . inserted for the sake of the smooth functioning of the apparatus.

3. Fromm's sketchy attempts to come up with a convincing alternative to this kind of directionless freedom were not successful. They were colored by the same one-sided antiauthoritarian bent that caused much of the problem in the first place (Richardson et al., 1999, pp. 64–67). But his insights into the "ambiguity of freedom" that can make freedom "an unbearable burden" (1941/65, p. 53) are well worth revisiting.
4. Evidence for the erasure of this classical notion of liberty can be found by if one goggles the term "negative liberty." The Wikipedia entry for the term reads: "**Negative liberty** is freedom from interference by other people. Negative liberty is primarily concerned with freedom from external restraint and contrasts with **positive liberty** (the possession of the power and resources to fulfill one's own potential)." In other words, it seems to be commonsense that one has to choose either (1) arbitrary authority or domination or (2) instrumental prowess in the service of a narrowly personal self-actualization on the other.
5. Deneen (2018) suggests that this liberal faith represents one of the three major political ideologies of modern times, the other two being communism and fascism. The

cultural historian Jackson Lears (2017) suggests that the terms liberal democracy and liberal individualism "capture the tension between individual freedom and communal well-being that has animated American politics since the nation's founding."

6. As the upsurge of psychotherapeutic activities in American society was just getting underway, the distinguished researcher Paul Meehl (1959) expressed a sharp concern that therapists would behave like "crypto-missionaries" (p. 257) seeking to convert their clients to their own preferred cultural, moral, or religious values. Slife et al. (2003) point out that it was to prevent just this sort of thing from happening that the psychology field adopted an ideal of value neutrality. Just as "good scientists are assumed to be objective and value-free observers of psychological facts, good therapists are assumed to be objective and value-free observers of therapeutic facts."

   However, dozens of research studies on values and therapy over years confirm that counseling and psychotherapy are anything but value-neutral (Beutler & Bergan, 1991; Kelly & Strupp, 1992; Tjeltveit, 1986, 1999). Some of the most interesting findings concern what has been come to be known as "value convergence" between therapist and client over the course of therapy. Slife et al. (2003, p. 63) argue that this research shows that value convergence "is even more important to therapy improvement than a host of other factors, such as therapist credibility and competence." As a matter of fact, "all sorts of values seem to be important to perceived client improvement—professional values, moral values, and in many studies religious values were pivotal." But what is this convergence? It might sound "like a mutual and reciprocal relationship between client and therapist." However, it does not appear to be an innocent blending of perspectives. "Overwhelming, this research indicates that therapists do not change their values during therapy; only clients change their values." One might say that therapists only perceive success in therapy when their clients have come to have values like their own (Tjeltveit, 1986). The basis for saying this lies in evidence indicating that "values convergence . . . does not apply to client's ratings of their own improvement; it only applies to therapists' rating of improvement and normality" (Slife et al., 2003, p. 64). So, one might ask, are we talking about value "convergence" or value "conversion" the very thing Meehl feared in the 1950s?

7. Unfortunately, Frank gives few suggestions as to how we might synthesize, let us say, self-restraint or finding meaning in suffering with the aggressive modern pursuit of health, success, and "individual self-fulfillment." As a matter of fact, a primary focus on individual self-fulfillment and the possibly neglected traditional values Frank mentions seem like mutually exclusive alternatives. Frank is a highly regarded and honored scholar in psychology and more broadly. Still, very few in psychology pay any attention to the problems in psychology he has written about for many years. They may give a nod to his unusually rich historical account and then just go about their conventional business. Perhaps putting him up on a pedestal, which he certainly deserves, is an effective way of deflecting his troubling criticisms of their field. I met him late in his life and found him to be a deeply sincere and most admirable individual. But he seemed painfully perplexed about how the field or his own reflections might credibly progress.

8. This historical and critical perspective on the stress idea and research is particularly interesting to someone like myself who began his career in academic psychology working on that topic, including publishing a book entitled *Stress, Sanity, and Survival* (Woolfolk & Richardson, 1978). At the time, it seemed to us like there was no more worthwhile undertaking than developing ways that ordinary citizens, not just therapy patients, might reduce stress in a beleaguered modern society .

9. Again, it seems very important to me to indicate that "liberalism" should mean "liberal individualism," a set of ideals and institutions that blends indispensable values of human dignity and equal worth with an ever more corrosive self-seeking, the latter bound to undermine the former over time.

References

Bandura, A. (1969). *Principles of behavior modification.* New York: Holt, Rinehart & Winston.

Bell, D. (1978). *The cultural contradictions of capitalism.* New York: Basic Books.

Becker, D. (2013). One nation under stress: The trouble with stress as an idea. United Kingdom: Oxford University Press.

Bellah, Robert, Richard Madsen, William Sullivan, Ann Swindler, and Steven Tipton. (1985). Habits of the Heart. Berkeley: University of California Press.

Bernstein, R. (1983). *Beyond objectivism and relativism.* Philadelphia: University of Pennsylvania Press.

Bernstein, R. J. (1976). *The restructuring of social and political theory.* Philadelphia: University of Pennsylvania Press.

Bishop, Robert C. (2007). *The Philosophy of the Social Sciences: An Introduction.* New York: Continuum.

Brooks, D. (2018, June 14). Personalism: The philosophy we need. *New York Times.*

Beutler, L., and Bergan, J. (1991). Value change in counseling and psychotherapy: A search for scientific credibility. *Journal of Consulting and Clinical Psychology,* 43, 16–24.

Cooper, C. L., & Dewe, P. (2004). *Stress: A brief history.* Malden, MA: Blackwell Publishing. https://doi.org/10.1002/9780470774755PsycINFO

Christopher, J. (1999). Counseling's inescapable moral visions. *Journal of Counseling & Development,* 75, 17–25.

Coles, R. (1987). Civility and psychology. In Bellah, R., Madsen, R. Sullivan, W., Swindler, A., & Tipton, S., (Eds.). *Individualism and Commitment in American Life.* New York: Harper and Row.

Cushman, Philip. (1990). "Why the Self is Empty." *American Psychologist,* 45: 599–611.

Deneen, P. (2018). *Why liberalism failed.* New Haven, CT: Yale University Press

Embra, C. (2018, April 6). Liberalism is loneliness. *Washington Post.*

Fancher, Robert. (1995). *Cultures of Healing: Correcting the Image of American Mental Health Care.* New York: W. H. Freeman and Company.

Fowers, B. (2005). *Virtue ethics and psychology: Pursuing excellence in ordinary practices.* Washington, DC: APA Press Books.

Frank, J. (1978). *Psychotherapy and the human predicament.* New York: Schocken.

Fromm, E. (1965). *Escape from freedom.* New York: Avon (Original work published in 1941).

Fromm, E. (1975). *Man for himself.* New York: Fawcett Premier (Original work published in 1947).

Fowers, B. (2005). *Virtue ethics and psychology: Pursuing excellence in ordinary practices.* Washington, D. C.: APA Press Books.

Gadamer, H-G. (1981). *Reason in the age of science*. Cambridge, MA: MIT Press.

Gergen, K. (1982). *Toward transformation in social knowledge*. New York: Springer-Verlag.

Gergen, K. (1985). The social constructionist movement in modern psychology. *American Psychologist, 40*, 266–275.

Habermas, J. (1973). *Theory and practice*. Boston, MA: Beacon Press.

Habermas, J. (1991). *The philosophical discourse of modernity*. Cambridge, MA: The MIT Press.

Hacking, I. (2007-). *Historical ontology*. Cambridge, MA: Harvard University Press.

Hauerwas, S. (1977). *Truthfulness and tragedy: Further investigations in Christian ethics*. Notre Dame, IN: University of Notre Dame Press.

Havel, V. (1995, March). Forgetting we are not God. *First Things*, 47–50.

Held, D. (1980). *Introduction to critical theory: Horkheimer to Habermas*. Berkeley, CA: University of California Press.

Hoffman, I. Z. (1996). The intimate and ironic authority of the psychoanalyst's presence. *Psychoanalytic Quarterly, 65*, 102–136.

Horkheimer, M. (1974). *Eclipse of reason*. New York: Continuum (First published in 1947).

Hoy D. (1986). Power, repression, progress. In D. Hoy (Ed.), Foucault: A critical reader (pp. 123–147). New York: Basil Blackwell.

Hutmacher, F. (2019). On the Janus-facedness of stress and modern life. *Journal of Theoretical and Philosophical Psychology, 39*(3), 181–192. http://doi.org/10.1037/teo0000113

Kelly, T., & Strupp, H. (1992). Patient and therapist values in psychotherapy: Perceived changes, assimilation, similarity, and outcome. *Journal of Consulting and Clinical Psychology, 60*, 34–40.

Kolakowski, L. (1986, June 16). The idolatry of politics. *The New Republic*, pp. 29–36.

Kugelmann, R. (1992). *Stress: The nature and history of engineered grief*. Westport, CT: Praeger.

Lasch, C. (1995). *The revolt of the elites and the betrayal of democracy*. New York: W. W. Norton.

Lears, J. (2017, Fall). Technocratic vistas: The long con of neoliberalism. *The Hedgehog Review, 19*.

Lippmann, W. (1993). *The phantom public*. New York: Routledge (Original work published in 1925).

Lippmann, W. (2022). *Public opinion*. Greenwood, WI: Suzeteo Enterprises (Original work published 1922).

McCarthy, T. (1978). *The critical theory of Jürgen Habermas*. Cambridge, MA: MIT Press.

MacIntyre, A. (1981). *After virtue*. Notre Dame: University of Notre Dame Press.

Meehl, P. E. (1959). Some technical and axiological problems in the therapeutic handling of religious and valuational material. *Journal of Counseling Psychology, 6*(4), 255–259.

Moon, J. D. (1983). Political ethics and critical theory. In D. Sabia & J. Wallulis (Eds.), *Changing social science* (pp. 171–188). Albany, NY: SUNY Press.

Neal, Patrick. (1990). "Justice as Fairness." *Political Theory*, 18: 24–50.

Nhat Hanh, T. (2021). *Zen and the art of saving the planet*. London: Rider Books.

Pollock, K. (1988). On the nature of social stress: Production of a modern mythology. *Social Science and Medicine, 26*, 381–392. https://doi.org/10.1016/0277-9536(88)90404-2

Rawls, John. (1971). *A Theory of Justice*. Cambridge, MA: Harvard University Press.

Richardson, F., & Fowers, B. (1998). Interpretive social science: An overview. *American Behavioral Scientist, 41*, 465–495.

Richardson, F., Fowers, B., & Guignon, C. (1999). *Re-envisioning psychology: Moral dimensions of theory and practice*. San Francisco, CA: Jossey-Bass Publishers.

Richardson, F., & Manglos, N. (2012). Rethinking instrumentalism. *Journal of Consciousness Studies, 19*, 177–201.

Root, M. (1993). *Philosophy of social science*. Oxford: Blackwell.

Rosa, H. (2010). Alienation and acceleration. Towards a critical theory of late-modern temporality. Malmö, Sweden: NSU Press.

Rosa, H. (2013). *Social acceleration: A new theory of modernity*. New York: Columbia University Press. https://doi.org/10.7312/rosa14834

Sandel, M. (1996). *Democracy's discontent: America in search of a public philosophy*. Cambridge, MA: Belknap/Harvard.

Sarason, S. (1986). And what is the public interest? *American Psychologist, 41*, 899–905.

Selznick, Philip. (1992). *The Moral Commonwealth: Social Theory and the Promise of Community*. Berkeley: University of California Press.

Selznick, P. (1998). Foundations of communitarian liberalism. In A. Etzioni (Ed.), *The essential communitarian reader* (pp. 3–14). Lanham, MD: Rowman & Littlefield Publishers.

Sennett, R. (1998). *The corrosion of character: The personal consequences of work in the new capitalism*. New York: Norton.

Sennett, R. (2006). *The culture of the new capitalism*. New Haven, CT: Yale University Press.

Slife, B., Smith, A., & Burchfield, C. (2003). Psychotherapists as crypto-missionaries: An exemplar on the crossroads of history, theory, and philosophy. In D. Hill & M. Krall (Eds.), *About psychology: At the crossroads of history, theory, and philosophy*. Albany, NY: State University of New York Press.

Sullivan, W. (1986). *Reconstructing public philosophy*. Berkeley: University of California Press.

Taylor, C. (1975). *Hegel*. Cambridge: Cambridge University Press.

Taylor, C. (1989). *Sources of the self*. Cambridge, MA: Harvard University Press.

Taylor, C. (1995). *Philosophical arguments*. Cambridge, Mass.: Harvard.

Tjeltveit, A. (1986). The ethic of value conversion in psychotherapy: Appropriate and inappropriate therapist on client values. *Clinical Psychology Review, 6*, 515–553.

Tjeltveit, A. C. (1999). *Ethics and values in psychotherapy*. London: Routledge.

Winch, P. (1958). *The idea of social science and its relation to philosophy*. London: Routledge & Kegan Paul.

Winch, P. (1977). Understanding a primitive society. In F. Dallmayr & T. McCarthy (Eds.), *Understanding and social inquiry* (pp. 159–188). Notre Dame, IN: University of Notre Dame Press.

Woolfolk, R., & Richardson, F. (1978). *Stress, sanity, and survival*. New York: Sovereign.

4 Early Religion and the Axial Age

The history of human suffering coincides with the history of the human race. But the meaning of suffering and beliefs about how to understand and best cope with it vary a great deal across eras and cultures. Perhaps the greatest shift in how these matters are viewed occurred during the period of time Karl Jaspers (1953/2021) famously dubbed the "Axial Age," from about 800 to 200 BCE. During this era, great revolutions in thought and sensibility seemingly emerged independently, given voice by such figures as the Hebrew prophets, Confucius, Socrates, the Taoist sages, and Buddha. These faiths and philosophies profoundly transformed our understanding of both the divine or transcendence and human flourishing. According to Charles Taylor (2007), in "early" or "archaic" religion the divine is "immanent in the cyclic rhythms of the natural world" and society is somehow enmeshed in these worldly processes; above all, people seek a "harmonious integration" of "human beings with the natural world" (p. 152). They deal with, beseech, or contend with spirits and forces that are "intricated in numerous ways in the world" (p. 150). Thus, what "people ask for when they invoke or placate divinities and powers is prosperity, health, fertility [and] to be preserved from . . . disease, dearth, sterility, premature death," and other evils (p. 150). Their sense of self was one of being "open and porous and vulnerable to a world of spirits and powers" (p. 27).

When I try to picture people seeking healing for many ills at early, premodern religious sites and shrines, I vividly recall drawings and photos I viewed as a youth with interest and puzzlement of multitudes gathering from all over the world at the Roman Catholic shrine of the Sanctuary of Our Lady of Lourdes in Lourdes, France. Many millions of petitioners and tourists have visited the shrine since 1859 when appearances there of the Blessed Virgin Mary were first recorded. The waters of a spring-fed grotto at Lourdes have been thought to have healing powers and many seemingly miraculous cures for vicarious diseases and conditions have been reported over the years.[1] I was struck by the images of distraught

DOI: 10.4324/9780203731840-5

individuals, often with pain-marked faces, some weeping, accompanied by family or friends, some carried or in wheelchairs, small groups of them in lines or side by side, seeking relief for ills that no other treatment had afforded.

This scene, discovered while rummaging through an encyclopedia, seemed very strange to me as an inquisitive kid from Toledo, Ohio, living in a comfortable home at a time when modern medicine seemed to take good care of many diseases and injuries. But even then, I believe, I sensed that a comfortable American existence obscured important aspects of human life. Dangers lurked, death loomed [like many children, more than many adults realize, I thought about death quite fearfully from time to time (Yalom, 1980)]. Looking back, it is not hard to feel a connection with the pilgrims at Lourdes or empathy with the supplicants of archaic religion. Their needful cries for help, their hope against hope in times of distress, reflect enduring human realities that we would rather not think about if and when it is possible to distract ourselves from doing so.

I recall a few years ago, when hospitalized for a condition that might have proved fatal, walking the halls for a little exercise in one of those flimsy hospital gowns, feeling like a waif, I glanced into the open doors of rooms as I passed by them. A number of times I saw someone leaving a room, a relative or visitor, gradually erase the pain and worry on their faces and replace them with a solemn, expressionless visage as they entered into the hall. It strikes me that if we patients and families were arrayed across the floor of an arena or large outside tent—which of course needs for privacy and sanitation would not allow—the honesty of our shared struggles and common humanity might afford a measure of acceptance and a bit of comfort, more than is available when closeted in medical cubicles, sad and disconnected from the rest of life.

Nevertheless, there are features of the understanding of life implicit in archaic religion that humans were bound eventually to question and rebel against. As Taylor (2007) describes it, in earlier societies people experience themselves as deeply embedded in society and the cosmos and as flourishing or languishing together as a community. The primary form of human agency is "the social group as a whole," as in collective ritual action. There, we "primarily relate to God as a society" (p. 148). Crucial roles in that activity are filled by priests, shamans, or chiefs and the "social order in which these roles were defined tended to be sacrosanct." Some thinkers of the radical Enlightenment pilloried this aspect of social and religious life, a lot of which still survived in early modern times, which seemed to entrench forms of inequality and domination. Thus they longed, in Voltaire's famous phrase, for the day when "the last king would be strangled with the entrails of the last priest" (p. 149).

A "Great Disembedding"

Axial Age faiths and philosophies were fashioned by sages and thinkers who plumbed the depths of human experience in a new way. They confronted the profound limits of human being indicated by inescapable suffering and mortality and felt deeply the search for a deeper and more lasting sense of meaning. As compared with earlier religion, Axial faiths and philosophies have a profound "quarrel with life" (Taylor, 2007, p. 153). For example, Huston Smith (1991, p. 101) writes that the "exact meaning" of the First Nobel Truth of the Buddha that life is Dukkha—usually but not entirely adequately translated "suffering"—is that, in his words, "Life (in the condition it has gotten itself into) is dislocated. Something has gone wrong. It is out of joint. As its pivot is not true, friction (interpersonal conflict) is excessive, movement (creativity) is blocked, and it hurts."[2]

It was a mistake of some Enlightenment thinkers to look back on Axial faiths and philosophies as simply naïve, irrational, or oppressive. The Axial Age transforms the picture of the world as enchanted with intra-cosmic spirits and causal powers inherent in things and cultivates a new understanding of our social existence. In fact, in Taylor's (2007) view, Axial faiths and philosophies all bring about a kind of radical new *individualism* through what he calls a "Great Disembedding." Society itself begins to be reconceived in a novel way as "made up of individuals" (Taylor, 2007, p. 146). Moreover, such individuals may be empowered in unprecedented ways to criticize their society in the light of new understandings of ultimate goods of justice and/or compassion, witness Socrates, the Hebrew prophets, the Buddha, Jesus of Nazareth, and others, many or most of whom were executed for their trouble. Taylor and others suggest that a modern sense of personal liberty, liberal democracy, and untrammeled scientific inquiry are in some ways an outgrowth of this shift.

The cornerstone of Axial Age views is a portrayal of the transcendent, at least in part, "as quite beyond or outside the cosmos," as Taylor (2007) points out is the case with both Jewish and Buddhist accounts (p. 152), their differences notwithstanding. Glenn Hughes (2003, p. 25) summarizes this turn toward transcendence in this way:

> In various cultures during this period, the quest for ultimate meaning led to experiential and conceptual breakthroughs in which the ground of human existence and the universe became explicitly recognized and symbolized as a reality beyond the conditions of space and time, and consequently unknowable in its essence by human beings.

Hughes (2003) gives several vivid examples of this turn toward transcendence. First, in classical Chinese culture, in the *Tao Te Ching*, attributed to the sage Lao-tzu around the sixth century B.C.E., ultimate reality is called the Tao, but the "reality itself is beyond naming and direct human understanding" (p. 25). A famous verse from the *Tao Te Ching* (Mitchell, 1988) puts it this way.

> The Tao that can be told
> Is not the eternal Tao.
> The name that can be named
> Is not the eternal name

Similarly, in Hindu culture, in the scriptures known as the Upanishads, developed around 800–200 B.C.E., "what is called Brahman is described as the one transcendent reality underlying and constituting the true being of all physical reality, all finiteness, all individuality" (Hughes, 2003, p. 26). Third, Yahweh, the God of the Hebrews, is proclaimed to be

> the sole divinity and fashioner of the universe, a divinity not to be identified with any aspect of the physical world.... All finite reality is regarded as a manifestation of God's unlimited freedom, a freedom in which human beings, alone among creatures, have been created to participate.

Because made in the image of God's unlimited freedom, the "limited free consciousness of human beings, through its questioning search for meaning and direction, allows for those experiences of transcendence that reveal the absolutely spiritual origin of human and worldly existence" (p. 27).

In addition, in classical Greek culture in the sixth through fourth centuries B.C.E., there emerges "distinctively *philosophical* symbols of transcendence." For example, in Plato's *Republic* Socrates asserts to his interlocutors that "everything that has being comes into being because of 'the Good' (*agathon*)" (Hughes, 2003, p. 27).

However, as the engendering source of all that has being, the Good itself "isn't being but is still beyond being, exceeding it in dignity and power" (The Republic of Plato, 509b). Hughes (2003, p. 28). comments that this

> intentionally paradoxical notion of a reality that is said to be "beyond being" conveys ... at once an idea of transcendent reality and the ... insight that such a reality lies beyond language and can be alluded to only through expressions that indicate their own inadequacy ("The Tao that can be told/is not the eternal Tao").

Finally, we might add that Buddhism, inaugurated by the Buddha in (probably) the later part of the fifth century B.C.E., represents another, distinctive Axial Age account of transcendence and our participation in it. Most schools of Buddhist thought do not deny the experience of a self, but only that it is a permanent, separate, unchanging entity that can provide a basis for identity and security. Suffering is caused by "sensual craving, craving for being and craving for non-being" (Nanamoli & Bodhi, 1995, pp. 9, 16). The solution for this condition is "giving up, relinquishing, letting go, and rejecting of [such] craving" (9, 17). Enlightenment consists in realizing that one is not such a solid, bounded entity [surely parallel to the "bounded, masterful self" (Cushman, 1990) of the modern world's individualistic outlook] but a facet of a vast "interbeing" or "dependent co-arising" (Nhat Hanh, 1995) in which every object or experience is profoundly interdependent with every other.[3]

Along with these new understandings of transcendence, there arise quite new conceptions of human flourishing. According to Taylor (2007, p. 151), with "Christianity or Buddhism, for instance . . . there is a notion of our good which goes beyond [ordinary] human flourishing, which we may gain even while failing utterly on the scales of human flourishing, even through such a failing (like dying young on a cross); or which involves leaving the field of flourishing altogether (ending the cycle of rebirth)." In Taylor's (2011, pp. 17–18) words, these affirmations of transcendence affirm a particular "complementary symbiosis of renunciation and flourishing." This fundamental movement of the mind or soul ought to be of keen interest to theoretical psychologists and moral philosophers, whatever their final assessment of it turns out to be. In such views, "renouncing, aiming beyond life, not only takes you away but also brings you back to flourishing." In the biblical tradition, it is unambiguously because of God's benevolent will that humans flourish. In Buddhist terms, "Enlightenment does not just turn you from the world," but also "opens the floodgates of *metta* (loving kindness) and *karuna* (compassion)." Suffering and loss are real and painful and cannot be softened or explained away. But this path, Taylor writes, can lead to "the insight that there can be in suffering and death not merely negation, the undoing of fullness and life, but also the affirmation of something which matters beyond life, on which life itself originally draws."

For example, Buddha's first sermon consists of the Four Noble Truths. (1) There is suffering. (2) The cause for suffering is either attachment to pleasure and possessions or aversion to pain and loss. (3) There is a way to end this suffering. (4) that way is the Eightfold Path, consisting of right views, right intent, right speech, right conduct, right livelihood, right effort, right mindfulness, and right concentration. Everything in Buddhist thought that we might call metaphysics or ethical theory grows out of and is meant to contribute to a resolute practical search for a kind of enlightenment which overcomes suffering and finds a better way of living in the world.

The contemporary Buddhist thinker Mark Epstein (1995) puts the insight expressed by the Second Nobel Truth in the following way:

> The ego, as subject, wishes to know itself securely but cannot and so is forced to pretend, not just to satisfy the demands of parents but to satisfy itself. In the attempt to preserve this illusion of security, the ego races back and forth between the two extremes of fullness and empti-ness, hoping that one or the other will provide the necessary refuge.
>
> (p. 70)

The solution for this fruitless vacillation between grasping and escape, or between an insecure grip on pleasure and a futile avoidance of pain, is the thoroughgoing transcending of such craving. Lawrence Christensen (1999, p. 43) describes how a major Buddhist tradition called "the Middle Way" (Garfield, 1995) emphasizes that nothing, including the self, stands alone but instead exists only in a "web of interconnectedness." This view does not deny the existence of the self, only that there is any intrinsic nature of self, any permanent, separate, unchanging self, with which to identify and to which one can cling or attach—such attachment and craving for being (or non-being) leading, of course, to suffering and dis-ease. Christensen writes,

> Although the absence of a permanent, fixed self is generally heralded as a foundation of the Buddha's teaching . . . it is not so much the self that Buddha encouraged one to relinquish but rather one's attachments to the *view* of a separate self. . . . Buddhism emphasizes not being attached to self or to no-self, to both, or to no view of the self.

Indeed, Christensen points out that the Buddha at times spoke positively about the self, saying for example; "The self, the dearest thing for man becomes an absolute value, which has to be preserved by all means and in preference to everything else. . . . Man should never give up the self" (Samyutta Nikaya, I, 41). However, one realizes that one is an "empty self" (*anatman*) that exists only as part of a vast web of interconnectedness or "interbeing," and best occupies one's proper place or path in that wider world through practices of mindfulness and compassion.

To give another example, the theologian Marcus Borg (1987, pp. 112–115) suggests that the path of transformation that Jesus of Nazareth lived and taught—summarized in the saying that whoever "loses his life will preserve it"—involves a dying of "the self as the center of its own concerns" and dying to "the world as the center of security and identity." This path or way involves a "central movement" of "handing over," "surrendering," or "letting go" and a radical centering in God or a "world of Spirit" that is *both* immanent in the world *and* radically transcends it. This in no way denies or depreciates the goods or enjoyments of ordinary life (as, for example, some strands of Gnosticism and other kinds of asceticism appear to have done). However, it makes them secondary to an ethical or spiritual path of living that is in one sense "higher" but nevertheless entails a life *in* this world of turning away from envy, anger, retribution, and violence to one of self-forgetful, forgiving love.

Axial faiths and philosophies open up the possibility of a new kind of response to suffering and evil. Jonathan Sacks (2005) the former Chief Rabbi of Great Britain and noted public intellectual terms this "transforming suffering." Sacks suggests that any credible view of transforming suffering will incorporate Victor Frankl's (1985) idea that the meaning of life is to be found "in the world rather than within [one's own] psyche . . . human existence is essentially self-transcendence rather than self-actualization" (quoted in Sacks, 2005, p. 221). In Sacks' (2005) words, "whether we are religious or irreligious, there is something we are *called on to do*, something no one else can do . . . not in these circumstances" (p. 219). This means that we have to make our way in a world in which we inescapably encounter some degree of pain, disappointment, heartbreak, loss, moments of real despair, and death. As Frankl put it, "Suffering is an eradicable part of life." This means that in a strange way then, "without suffering and death, human life cannot be complete." So, "if there is a meaning in life at all, there must be a meaning in suffering" (quoted in Sacks, 2005, p. 223).

Frankl and Sacks give voice to two ideas or insights that, if true, are of considerable importance. One is that even though we have to struggle to see situations clearly, fight through inclinations to avoid or escape uncomfortable realities, and think through the issues at hand as carefully as possible, in the end, in dealing with significant questions of meaning and morality we find ourselves more chosen than choosing. We find that we are eventually, in Frankl's words, "called" by some perspective or value we can't dismiss without doing great harm to our conscience or integrity. The other is that we have to pursue understanding and decide how to act in a world permeated with suffering and death, where dealing with suffering or death is frequently the matter at hand. The quality of Frank's (1985) reflections on these topics in books like *Man's Search for Meaning: An Introduction to Logotherapy*, based in part on his experiences in a Nazi concentration camp, helps explain why many books of psychology come and go but his can be found on the shelves of most bookstores and are still widely read.

An "Expanded View of Human Subjectivity"

A later chapter will discuss more fully how transforming suffering in this sense might make sense in a post-traditional world. At this point, however, it might be helpful to identify the main barrier to drawing on the possible wisdom of Axial age perspectives in this regard. Jeffrey Rubin (1996, 1997), who has written extensively on psychoanalysis and Buddhism, detects the problem. Rubin would agree that the critique of liberal individualism set out in the previous chapter. He concurs that what Philip Cushman (1990) terms the "bounded, masterful self" of modern imagination—which, coupled with a particular set of human rights makes up liberal individualism—is largely an illusion and a harmful one. Rubin (1997) argues that we need somehow *both* to preserve modern culture's affirmation of human dignity and rights *and* thoroughly revise the concept of a separate "I." He argues that we require an "expanded view of human subjectivity," which includes seriously reconsidering the viability of some traditional views of transcendence. To this end, He recommends that we explore the reality and importance of what he calls "non-self-centric states of being." In such states, "there is a nonpathological dedifferentiation of boundaries between self and world: a self-empowering sense of connection between self and world that results in a lack of self-preoccupation, a sense of timelessness, efficacy, and peace." Rubin adds, "[such] moments of non-self-centricity—whether surrendering, merging, yielding, letting go—seem to be part of most spiritual traditions" (p. 84). We need to think more "dialectically," he feels, and appreciate that self and other, person and world, *define* one another in essential respects and *permeate* one another's being.

There are a number of prominent philosophers and writers (Berger, 1979; Havel, 1985; Hughes, 2003; Long, 2006; Schwartz, 2004; Taylor, 2007, to mention just a few) and some theoretical psychologists (Freeman, 2014; Gantt & Williams, 2014; Richardson, 2014; Slife, 2014) who have sought, in Hughes (2003, p. 29) words, to "recover transcendence," or at least to make such a recovery seem possible and worth exploring. All of them would agree with Rubin (1997) that we need an expanded view of human subjectivity. Mainly what stands in the way of such a view and a possible recovery of transcendence is what Bellah et al. (1985) term "ontological individualism." We are inculcated into this sense of ourselves from birth. We tacitly tend to view human beings atomistically as discrete centers of experience and action concatenated in various ways into social groups, struggling to reduce inevitable conflicts with others mainly through negotiations and temporary alliances.

Few if any of us are pure ontological individualists. Most of us harbor some other values or ideals that are not merely chosen but have some authority for us and are important to us as part of our identity and essential to our self-respect as decent or good persons. These include such things as a sense of honor, an ability to forgive others at times, a sense of humility about our faults and limitations, generosity for its own sake, appreciation of our dependence on others or the past for personal qualities and opportunities we prize, loyalty to some others that goes beyond their usefulness to us, and a willingness at times to sacrifice for friends and family with no expectation of compensation or reward. They may also include an adoration of beauty in art or nature for its own sake, courage in the face of adversity, and some sense of reverence or the sacred. These meanings and values can afford persons with a sense of dignity and worth that can make suffering less destructive or more bearable and allow it to help clear away illusions and pretenses that stand in the way of greater wisdom about what is really important in life.

The problem is, however, that our liberal individualist credo, which combines ontological individualism with a set of inherent human rights, puts such meanings or values as these on a quite shaky footing. Liberal individualism's commitment to respecting the rights of others gives the appearance of protecting our prized individuality and moral autonomy because it only commands us to respect the right of others to choose any ends of their own consistent with *their* respecting the right of others to do the same. Otherwise, the content of the ends chosen is left to the individual. As we have seen, however, this view represents a dissonant and unstable blend of radical self-interest with a serious regard for the inviolable rights and dignity of others, where self-interest tends to erode our regard for others and make if quite difficult when they regularly clash for us to significantly suspend or compromise our personal wants or ends. As Tocqueville (1969/1835, p. 508) put it a number of years ago, individualistic Americans are inclined to think that they "owe no [one] anything and hardly expect anything from anybody," and "form the habit of thinking that their whole destiny is in their hands." Such people come to "forget their ancestors" and also their descendants. "[They] are forever thrown back on [themselves] alone, and there is danger that [they] may be shut up in the solitude of [their] own heart[s]."

The difficulty is even greater with values such as generosity, humility, and sacrifice for others.[4] These require a greater compromise of our narrow self-interest and ask us to identify with a way of being that is uncomfortably different in kind. Of course, this would not be as great a problem if we inhabited an expanded view of human subjectivity such that our greatest good overlapped or coincided in a basic way ontologically with the good of others or the common good of our communities—as parents commonly feel about their children, friends about friends, or non-jingoistic patriots about their country. We do feel that way sometimes, but there remains considerable tension between these commitments and our pressing need to rush ahead down the path toward greater success, control, and security in the world. We operate with a sharp dichotomy between "doing our own thing" and doing someone else's thing or being under their more or less oppressive thumb. We need to think of these other-regarding values and meanings not as something, in the end, that we are "called" to do but as something we *autonomously* choose for ourselves rather than not anchored in any way in wider or deeper realities. But then they are hard to explain to ourselves or others, hard to make a part of our reflection about any wider, shared social or political goods, and lose their meaning-giving force in both daily living and times of crisis. These difficulties and any doubt we may have about the goodness of our conventional goals only intensify when pain or suffering enters the picture.

When any sense or intimation of transcendence comes into play, these problems only magnify. To a modern soul, being asked by Socrates to consider orienting oneself to a reality "beyond being" that exceeds it in dignity and power can easily seem doubly preposterous. The modern self-contained or bounded, masterful self may see itself as having a rich inner life, full of possibilities. But it tends to view the objective, surrounding world as neutral or indifferent, to be described or explained in the main by the natural sciences. The idea of an enthralling reality beyond worldly being will appear to crush moral autonomy in a particularly brutal fashion and believing in it seem tantamount to believing once again in the tooth fairy.

"Many Realities"

Peter Berger (1977, 1979) digs into some of the often unexamined assumptions of this modern outlook and suggests a fresh approach to questions concerning transcendence. Berger elucidates certain "dilemmas of modernity," by which he means particular features of modern life that expand human powers and enhance individual uniqueness, but also undercut the matrix of reliable social ties and shared meanings needed to support them. The most basic dilemma Berger identifies is brought about by our capability for "abstraction." Abstraction in his sense refers to our ability to detach ourselves or abstract away from the everyday experience of reality as "an ongoing flux of juncture and disjunction of unique entities," a flow of events and experiences that is often marked by unexpected turns of events and emotional surprises. Through the power of abstraction, we come to view events and even our own experiences and actions as separate components of formal, impersonal systems in which they are "continuously interdependent in a rational, controllable, predictable way" (p. 27).

In a similar vein, hermeneutic philosophy (Gadamer, 1989; Taylor, 1989) explores the consequences of this heavy stress on abstraction for an ontology of the human realm. By rejecting a traditional picture of the world as a cosmic dwelling suffused with meanings and purposes and adopting an approach that can be called abstraction and objectification (Richardson, Fowers, & Guignon, 1999, p. 202), early scientists could describe the world as a vast collection of neutral objects on hand for our theorizing and possibly technological control. This same approach also encourages an atomistic view of social reality as a collection of encapsulated individual "subjects."[5] The self appears as either a kind of thing in the world or a disengaged individual mind. Taylor (1993) describes this picture of things as resulting from an "ontologizing of method." It is assumed that *only* those things or events that can be represented and discussed by a quantifying and experimental approach to inquiry have objective reality. The rest or are little more than subjective whimsy.

Of course, the concrete everyday world of history and culture we inhabit, which we quite properly abstract away from for the purposes of natural science inquiry, is still very much with us. And what a world it is! Chock full of beauty, ugliness, mystery, brute physicality, stunning creativity, moral values and purposes, noble sacrifices, evil acts, experiences of both profound love and connection with others incredibly painful alienation from them, overwhelming loss, religious experiences of all kinds, peace of mind, emotional torment, crushing boredom, genuine ecstasy, terrible suffering, sometimes finding meaning in suffering, and much more. Many of the shortcomings of the social sciences can be traced to treating this world as merely a neutral, objective realm of events (Bishop, 2007; Richardson et al., 1999; Slife, 2004).

In his book *The Heretical Imperative: Contemporary Possibilities of Religious Affirmation*, Peter Berger (1979, pp. 66 ff.) applies this view to understanding transcendence. Berger points out that the word "heresy" derives from a Greek word meaning choice. In our contemporary pluralistic situation, he points our, we are surrounded by many different religious "orthodoxies." If religiously inclined or perhaps just curious, we may be drawn to several of them at once. It is no longer a matter of remaining orthodox or choosing against it. Rather, we are compelled to choose among a number of options for belief, with at least some uncertainty about the choice. Berger argues that this circumstance leads some theologies of radical transcendence to recommend making a particular kind of "leap of faith." He suggests that such an approach to transcendence presupposes a tacit acceptance of what he terms the "modern situation," namely a world shorn of most meanings and values by way of our great capacity for abstraction. The only option for religious affirmation, then, is to "leap" out of this situation into a realm of faith and meaning quite beyond or apart from this world. However, Berger argues that even if we could justify making such a leap into the dark or unknown, which he thinks is not plausible, how could we then determine in what direction to leap? There simply is no non-arbitrary way to decide upon or affirm any one among many possibilities, some indeed quite repugnant.

Berger (1979, pp. 36–41) suggests another approach to experiences of transcendence. He employs the phenomenologist and "interpretive sociologist" Alfred Schutz's idea of "many realities." In this view, "Reality is not experienced as one unified whole" but as "containing zones or strata with greatly differing qualities." The *paramount* reality, experienced as "more real *most of the time*," is "everyday waking consciousness." This is the "reality of being awake in ordinary, everyday life." In our day, this reality tends to be seen as filled with active, often instrumental activity set over against a neutral or impersonal universe. Paradoxically, this reality is both "massively real" and "very precarious." At a moment's notice, its accent of reality may diminish or vanish in an "experience of rupture." One finds oneself in a quite different zone or reality, in dreams, hallucinatory experiences, a world of pain or pleasure or ecstasy (as anyone knows who has ever been madly in love)," a world of "theoretical abstraction," or an "experience of the comic" in which the world appears "flawed, absurd, or even illusionary." In each case, "another world," with another sense of one's "true self" in it, is now paramount.

One of those other worlds appears in the religious experience of mystics. (At least fragments and flickers of such experiences occur in a great many people.) Generalizing across many such experiences, Berger (1979, pp. 42–43) suggests they open a kind of sacred space that "is perceived as having been there all along, though it was not previously perceived." Now, instead of any religious ideas or sentiments one might harbor being perceived as located in a corner of one's ordinary self or mind, the whole world of ordinary life is now seen as a small "antechamber" in a wider field of meaning and being. There "the sacred is experienced as being utterly other" and "is experienced as being of immense and indeed redemptive significance for human beings." Also, it "implies a different perception of other human beings and one's relation with them," often involving "a sense of intense connection or love." Berger's (1979) analysis is very much in line with Gabriel Marcel's (1973) view that in religious experience we behold a world "which is not superimposed from without ours, but is rather this very world grasped in a richness of dimensions which ordinarily we are simply unaware of."

Marcus Borg (1987, p. 43) quotes the Hindu poet Rabindranath Tagore, who writes about an experience that combines transformed cognition and joy. It reflects most of the qualities Berger summarizes.

> I suddenly felt as if some ancient mist had in a moment lifted from my sight and the ultimate significance of things was laid bare. . . . Immediately I found the world bathed in a wonderful radiance with waves of beauty and joy swelling on every side. And no person or thing in the world seemed to me trivial or unpleasing.[6]

Every vision or articulation of this kind is shaped by the culture in which it occurs and by the unique experiences and language of the visionary. Also, such experiences are grounded, ultimately, in the mystery of being. Thus, Borg (1998) asserts that all of our concepts and images of God "are attempts to express the ineffable," an ineffable in which "we live and move and have our being" but which remains "beyond all our concepts, even this one" (p. 49). In the famous phrase of St. Paul, we "see through a glass darkly." This view of things, rightly understood, would seem to undercut any conception of God or transcendence as an "absolute monarch set over against the world" (Long, 1998, p. 4) that suppresses human moral autonomy and responsibility. It undermines the sort of dogmatic religion that insists on the finality and certainty of its beliefs. All we have is a vision or perception of things like Tagore's. "All" does not do it justice, however, because it brings for a time a fulfilling sense of meaning, belonging, and peace. Later many questions, even doubt, are very likely to arise, Berger notes, but at that time one inhabits a different world that is taken to be quite real.

The widely read pundit and author David Brooks (2019) describes his recent turn to religious faith in terms that are congruent with Berger's account. It was not, he states, a dramatic event, as in "A blinding light appeared! A voice called forth!" (p. 211). In fact, he writes, it "was not a religious conversion. . . . It felt more like deeper understanding . . . a sensation of opening my eyes to see what was always there, seeing the presence of the sacred in the realities of the everyday" (p. 233). He relates that:

> Walking near by a lake near the top of a mountain near Aspen, Colorado, reading a book of Puritan prayers he had brought with him, I had a sensation of things clicking into place, like the sound of a really nice car door gently closing. It was a sensation of deep harmony and membership . . . that creation is a living thing, a good thing, that we are all still being created and we are accepted in it . . . that there is an animating spirit underlying all creation. . . . After my hike up to American Lake, I realized I was a religious person.
>
> (pp. 232–234)

He adds:

> Rabbi [Abraham] Heschel says that awe is not an emotion; it is a way of understanding. "Awe is itself an act of insight into a meaning greater that ourselves." And I find that these days I can't see people except as en-souled creatures. I can't do my job as a journalist unless I start with the premise that all people have souls, and all the people I meet do, too.
>
> (p. 232)

In a chapter entitled "The Heritage of The Axial Age," Robert Bellah (2012) ponders the question of whether that heritage is a "resource" or a "burden" in facing the challenges of today's post-traditional world. Reasonable people disagree about the matter. It is Bellah who says a "heritage of explosive potentialities for good and for evil" (p. 465). Notions of radical transcendence like Plato's vision of the Good that is beyond being or the Old Testament's affirmation of Yahweh as the only God and creator of the universe can be seized upon to support one's claims to political domination and authority (obvious examples being the assertion of the divine rights of king and more or less harsh patriarchies) or to authorize one's supposedly incontestable moral or religious truths (as in the kinds of religious fundamentalism that obscure how their "literal" depiction of scripture are in fact highly tendentious and at least contestable interpretations of the same). Or they may nourish a sense of being only a small part of a wider, exceedingly meaningful, field of being, grounded ultimately in mystery, inspiring much humility, a great reluctance to judge others, and a love of neighbor, even the neighbor who seeks to do one harm. All I would insist on is that this dimension of life and experience has to be taken seriously—which means neither flippantly dismissed nor wrapped in dogmatic certainty—in pondering the meaning of human suffering.

Notes

1. Even though, no surprise, many scientific investigations have failed to find anything remarkable or curative about those waters.
2. Thus, these views take account of what Glenn Tinder (1981) terms our enormous, enduring "physical and metaphysical vulnerability" as humans (p. 21), namely a vulnerability to suffering and death and a worrying uncertainty as to what sort of meaning to find in or direction to give to our small lives. Tinder also argues that although it takes different forms in different times and places, many people and societies respond to this vulnerability by seeking to control or dominate nature and other humans. They remain blind to "the full reality of the entities they wish to control" and to "their own imperfections and perversities" (p. 90), leading ultimately to defeat of their efforts to dominate and to unanticipated, destructive consequences.
3. Here I can only gesture at this kind of subtle and profound Buddhist metaphysics. A fine introduction to this view can be found (Duckworth, 2011) in the teachings of the brilliant Tibetan monk, mystic, and philosopher Jamgon Mipam (1846–1912).
4. I have been struck by how often when college student are asked for examples of meaningful sacrifice in general or their own experience, they mention the care and devotion they have received from their parents.
5. We have to turn to a great artist for such a vivid account of this situation as Iris Murdoch (1970) provides. She describes this notion of personhood as

> the old substantial picture of the "self" . . . an isolated principle of will, or a burrowing principle of consciousness, inside, or beside, a lump of being which has been handed over to other disciplines. . . . On the one hand a Luciferan philosophy of adventures of the will, and on the other natural science.

6. To give another example, Borg (1987, pp. 43–51) quotes these lines from William Butler Yeats' poem "Vacillation."

> My fiftieth year had come and gone,
> I sat, a solitary man, in a crowded London shop,
> An open book and empty cup

On the marble table top.
While on the shop and street I gazed,
My body of a sudden blazed;
And twenty minutes more or less
It seemed, so great my happiness,
That I was blessed and could bless.

References

Bellah, R., Madsen, R., Sullivan, W., Swindler, A., & Tipton, S. (1985). *Habits of the heart: Individualism and community in American life*. Berkeley: University of California Press.

Bellah, R. (2012). The heritage of the axial age. In R. Bellah (Ed.), *The axial age and its consequences* (pp. 447–468). Cambridge, MA: The Belknap Press of Harvard University Press. https://doi.org/10.4159/harvard.9780674067400.c18

Berger, P. (1977). *Facing up to modernity*. New York: Basic Books.

Berger, P. (1979). *The heretical imperative*. Garden City, NY: Anchor Press/Doubleday.

Bishop, R. (2007). *The philosophy of the social sciences*. New York: Continuum.

Borg, M. (1987). *The God we never knew*. San Francisco: Harper/San Francisco.

Borg, M. (1998). *The God we never knew: Beyond dogmatic religion to a more authentic faith*. New York: HarperOne.

Brooks, D. (2019). *The second mountain: The quest for a moral life*. New York: Random House.

Christensen, L. (1999). *Suffering and the dialectical self in Buddhism and relational psychoanalysis. The American Journal of Psychoanalysis, 59*, 37–56.

Cushman, P. (1990). Why the self is empty. *American Psychologist, 45*, 599–611.

Duckworth, D. (2011). *Jamgon Mipam: His life and teachings*. Boston: Shambhala.

Epstein, M. (1995). *Thoughts without a thinker: Psychotherapy from a Buddhist perspective*. New York: Basic Books.

Frankl, V. (1985). *Man's search for meaning*. New York: Washington Square Press.

Freeman, M. (2014). Listening to the claims of experience: Psychology and the question of transcendence. *Pastoral Psychology, 63*(3), 323–337.

Gadamer, H.-G. (1989). *Truth and method* (2nd revised ed., J. Weinsheimer & D. Marshall, Trans.). New York: Crossroad.

Gantt, E., & Williams, R. (2008). Explaining religion to death: Reductionism, evolution, and the psychology of religion. *Issues in Religion and Psychotherapy, 32*, 3–13.

Gantt, E. E., & Williams, R. N. (2014). Psychology and the legacy of Newtonianism: Motivation, intentionality, and the ontological gap. *Journal of Theoretical and Philosophical Psychology, 34*(2), 83–100.

Garfield, J. (1995). *Mulamadhyamakakarika (The wisdom of the Middle Way)*. New York: Oxford.

Havel, V. (1985, March). Forgetting we are not God. *First Things*, 47–50.

Hughes, G. (2003). *Transcendence and history: The search for ultimacy from ancient societies to postmodernity*. Columbia, MO: Missouri University Press.

Jaspers, K. (2021). *The origin and goal of history*. New York: Routledge (Original work published in 1953).

Long, E. (1998). Quest for transcendence. *The Review of Metaphysics, 52,* 3–19.

Majjhima Nikaya (The middle length discourses of the Buddha). (1995). (B. Nanamoli & B. Bodhi, Trans.). Boston, MA: Wisdom Publications.

Marcel, G. (1973). *Tragic Wisdom and beyond* (S. Jolin & P. McCormiock, Trans.). Evanston: Northwestern University Press.

MItchell, S. (Trans.). (1988). *Tao Te Ching.* New York: Harper and Row.

Murdoch, I. (1970). *The sovereignty of Good.* London: Routledge & Kegan Paul.

Nhat Hanh, T. (1995). *Living Buddha, living Christ.* New York: Riverhead.

Richardson, F., Fowers, B., & Guignon, C. (1999). *Re-envisioning psychology: Moral dimensions of theory and practice.* San Francisco, CA: Jossey-Bass.

Richardson, F. (2014). Investigating psychology and transcendence. *Pastoral Psychology, 63,* 355–365.

Rubin, J. (1996). *Psychoanalysis and Buddhism: Toward an integration.* New York: Plenum Press.

Rubin, J. (1997). Psychoanalysis is self-centered. In C. Spezzano & G. Garguilo (Eds.), *Soul on the couch: Spirituality, religion, and morality in contemporary psychoanalysis.* Hillsdale, NJ: Analytic Press.

Sacks, J. (2005). *To heal a fractured world: The ethics of responsibility.* New York: Schocken Books.

Samyutta Nikaya (The book of the kindred sayings). (1994). (F. Woodward, Trans.). Oxford: Pali Text Society (first published in 1930).

Schwartz, B. (2004). *The paradox of choice: Why more is less.* New York: Harper-Collins.

Slife, B. (2004). Taking practices seriously: Toward a relational ontology. *Journal of Theoretical and Philosophical Psychology, 24,* 179–195.

Slife, B. (2014). Questioning the presumption of naturalism in the social sciences: A case study. *Pastoral Psychology, 63,* 339–353.

Smith, H. (1991). *The world's religions.* San Francisco, CA: HarperCollins.

Taylor, C. (1989). *Sources of the self.* Cambridge, MA: Harvard University Press.

Taylor, C. (1993). Engaged agency, and background in Heidegger. In C. Guignon (Ed.), *The Cambridge companion to Heidegger* (pp. 317–336). Cambridge: Cambridge University Press.

Taylor, C. (2007). *A secular age.* Cambridge, MA: Belknap Press of Harvard University Press.

Taylor, C. (2011). *Dilemmas and connections: Selected essays.* Cambridge, MA: Belknap Press of Harvard University Press.

Tinder, G. (1981). Against fate: An essay on personal dignity. *Notre Dame,* Indiana: University of Notre Dame Press.

Tocqueville, A. de. (1969). *Democracy in America.* New York: Anchor Books (Original work published 1835).

Yalom, I. (1980). *Existential psychotherapy.* New York: Basic Books.

5 Modern Approaches

In recent centuries, Western societies have made astounding advances in freedom, human rights, and science. These improvements have paved the way to unprecedented affluence, health and longevity, and many more opportunities for individual success and self-expression. There are still far too many people tragically left behind, but there has been an enormous expansion of opportunities for leading longer, richer lives marked by greater personal dignity and somewhat less marred by pain, disease, oppression, fear, and despair. No one who appreciates human life in any form or fashion can gainsay these blessings.

As Taylor (1989) points out, one of the major themes of contemporary Western civilization is a commitment to reducing avoidable and unjust human suffering. However, a cloud of ambiguity hangs over these achievements. As discussed in Chapter 3, they transpire in a cultural universe whose pubic philosophy to a great extent is liberal individualism where the guiding ethical ideal for many is the "affirmation of ordinary life." Unfortunately, this moral and political outlook throws serious roadblocks in the path of coming to terms with inescapable human suffering and adds new kinds of pain and suffering in its own right.

Eradicating Suffering and Its Causes

The most common approach to suffering in modern times views it exclusively or mainly as a disease to be cured or a condition to be set right. Most of us share a commitment to the straightforward eradication of the physical and social conditions that cause undue physical or emotional pain and suffering, to the fullest extent possible. Taylor (1989) observes that a principal value of contemporary Western society is a commitment to reduce human suffering. We pursue this goal through enhancing individual freedom (including civil rights) and emancipating individuals from lack of opportunity or oppression, leading to "remarkable opportunities for travel, diverse

DOI: 10.4324/9780203731840-6

cultural experiences, an enhanced sense of individual uniqueness, a greater awareness of our abilities and talents, and greater prospects for success." (Fowers, Richardson, & Slife, 2017, p. 158). We rejoice in the remarkable lifesaving and life-enhancing medical advances of the last 150 or so years. (Indeed, neither I, my wife, our children, or a number of our best friends and valuable colleagues would have survived into adulthood if we had been born a 150 years ago.)

Yet this very increased freedom and opportunity can induce relatively new kinds of debilitation and suffering. Schwartz (2004) refers to one of these as the "paradox of choice." It occurs when we are dumbfounded in the face of 10 or 20 choices between varieties of dish soap or decisions encumbered by dozens of minor options. (I remember the instructor in the first psychology course I took in the late 1950s describing a new client of his who experienced an emotional breakdown triggered by paralysis when confronted with over a dozen choices of toothpaste at a local drugstore I knew well. It struck me at the time as fascinating and somehow important, although then I had no idea why.) Schwartz has conducted clever experiments showing, for example, that individuals presented with 10 or more options for investing their retirement benefits chose to save less than those presented with only three or four. Such findings are suggestive, although Schwartz has little to say about how or on what basis we might set needed limits to reduce the burden of autonomy. More and more choices continue to beckon.

The problem is, our deep appreciation for the benefits accruing from increased freedom and scientific and technological progress notwithstanding, the human condition remains much the same. Advertising of all sorts celebrates and promises products and experiences that will bring us relief from pain and worry, a calm and placid existence, and many unambiguous pleasures and delights. Thus, it seems to many as if we now live or are close to living in a "technological Eden" (Rieff, 1966, p. 93). But at some point the bubble will burst. Our lives remain frail, vulnerable, and mortal, subject to many disappointments, heartbreaks, uncertainties, unanticipated and painful turns of events, and prone to considerable worry and anxiety about if and when these things might befall us or our children. And they do befall us more or less, even if rarely exactly in the form we feared they might. Many still suffer greatly and in the real world no one escapes pain, fear, acute disappointment, or being the object of malice or evil in some form during their lives. Everyone has to face their own death and the loss of dear ones, sometimes the suffering and death of a child.

It's hard to face these limitations and frailties when our only approach to suffering is to reduce or eliminate it at all costs. We may latch fervently onto the tools and toys of advanced medicine and technology and rush ahead like teenagers who feel like they are going to live forever. But the awareness of our vulnerability lurks somewhere, leading easily to some degree of obsessive denial of our condition. We often make a fetish of what influence or control we do possess, fall into a sense of victimization and blame ourselves, others, or God for the harm or misfortune that comes our way, or proclaim a sense of entitlement as a kind of magic potion that might protect against insult and injury. We may even sense the need for some greater wisdom about coming to terms with suffering, but we typically draw a blank as to what that might be.

In addition, there are peculiar ways in which some of our technological and social advances create new kinds of pain and difficulty and can intensify suffering. For example, Schumaker (2001) argues that a number of "mega-trends" in modern society cause considerable difficulty by cutting against the grain of our deeply social nature. Modernity drastically "detradition-alizes the world and sets in motion multiple out-of-control processes that require constant cultural, political, and institutional innovation" (pp. 1–2). We tend to be a "disorganized dust of individuals who have been freed too much from all genuine social bonds" (p. 16). The result is a vulnerable "free-floating" and "ephemeral" structure of identity in a great many modern people (p. 14).

Schumaker (2001) argues that in more communitarian cultures individuals have access to and feel supported by "socially sanctioned identity templates" and have recourse to shared "cultural coping strategies" in times of loss, conflict, or moral confusion. He drives home the point that there is often a great price to be paid for this loss of shared meanings in a "do your own thing" world. Schumaker makes the interesting point that because they tend to be emotionally isolated with limited experience and resources, individuals have to innovate or devise on their own coping techniques, workable defenses, credible answers to ethical dilemmas, or convincing consoling or meaning-giving philosophical or religious beliefs. Excessive personal responsibility with limited resources is a virtual recipe for chronic emotional strain and idiosyncratic, unreliable coping, assuming one doesn't just withdraw into debilitating passivity and emotional "deadness" (p. 26). All of this increases suffering.[1]

Schumaker (2001, p. 53 ff.) contends that even if there were evidence for a genetic component of depression or antidepressant medications sometimes reduced its symptoms, that would not imply an "automatic causal link between depression and biological characteristics." Rather, he cites considerable evidence to suggest that a culture's shared meanings and more communitarian coping strategies can raise the threshold for depression very high for most people. For example, he reports on research indicating that at least 50 percent of women in our society experience "maternity blues" and approximately 20 percent go on to develop more serious postnatal depression. But among the Kipsigis people of Kenya, medical anthropologists can find no evidence whatsoever for postpartum depression. In that culture, a predictable pattern of practices, rituals, and gifts following childbirth mark out a "distinct culturally acknowledged postnatal period," one that "confirm[s] symbolically the new mother's elevated standing" in the community and indeed the cosmos, affords her "pampered social seclusion and mandated rest," and provides considerable assistance with her new responsibilities for a time from community members.

The anthropologist Juli McGruder (1999) has carried out research that offers support for this perspective. McGruder studied the families of schizophrenics in Zanzibar, from a largely Muslim population where many also still hold Swahili spirit-possession beliefs. She found that these beliefs usually did *not* stigmatize ill persons but prescribed many acts of kindness and support that kept them connected to family and community. There is no reason to think there is less incidence of schizophrenia in these communities. But a host of evidence [summarized by Watters (2010, p. 134 ff.)] suggests that the course and outcome of the disease there and in many other developing countries is more favorable—less severe, longer periods of remission, higher levels of social functioning, and less permanent severe impairment—than in industrialized nations.

Living in a technologically advanced, pluralistic, relatively free society provides many of us with remarkable opportunities for travel, diverse cultural experiences, an enhanced sense of individual uniqueness, a greater awareness of our abilities and talents, and some degree of success in all sorts of commercial, professional, and artistic pursuits. However, this situation does nothing to erase fundamental human limitations of many sorts. More opportunities for fulfillment and success means that many, with regret, will have to be relinquished. Also, in a highly competitive world, there are always others who have more or do better, making it difficult not to be regularly afflicted with envy and self-doubt. One has to struggle hard to gain a reasonable measure of security and success, all the while being uncertain about and having frequently to rethink what is really worth striving for.

Of course, most of us moderns would find life in more traditional, only gradually changing ways of life far too conformist and confining, for a number of very good reasons. We would not want to go back even if we could. But we tend not to acknowledge the extent to which the course of events in which our lives are caught up is unpredictable, full of surprising turns of events, and to a significant extent simply not under our control. The ad for a popular new line of American cars simply shows one speeding down the highway and voices like a mantra, "True comfort is being fully in control." (Watch television for a few hours and one will encounter many different versions of this message and promise.) Besides being a vulgar sentiment, it is wildly out of touch with reality. Politicians and commentators demand of one another and excoriate one another for not having highly developed visions, plans, and programs for successful, nearly error-free, economic and political affairs and military undertakings. Of course, we need to do the best we can at anticipating and preparing for opportunities and difficulty, and there is authentic purpose and satisfaction in doing so. But looking back five years from any point in time one will be astonished at how much has transpired that could never have been imagined, both good and bad, both in one's personal life and in the wider world of culture and politics. Fantasies of excessive and impossible instrumental control over events only foster fear, cynicism, anger, and blaming, indeed endless blaming of others or oneself, which only work to undermine genuine responsibility and achieving such good outcomes that might be possible.

A one-sided, unending, unrealistic stress on eliminating suffering and its causes seems to be a clear example of the kind of veneration of instrumental reason, as discussed in Chapter 3, that the Frankfurt School and critical theorists from Horkheimer to Habermas (Held, 1980; McCarthy, 1978) held to be a major blind spot in modern culture, substituting a sheer increase in mastery or control to the neglect of other important, even preeminent meanings and values. Once again, Jerome Frank (1978), one of the most distinguished figures in the world of psychology and psychotherapy that burgeoned in the decades after World War II identified some of those meanings and values in his view as "the redemptive power of suffering, acceptance of one's lot in life, adherence to tradition, self-restraint and moderation" (pp. 6–7). In Chapter 3, also, I argued that liberal individualism (Sandel, 1996) or liberal voluntarism (Deneen, 2018), which appears to be almost the official credo of modern society tends to undermine its own best values of human dignity and rights and leave little in the way of purpose or direction for human action other than security and ordinary sorts of pleasure, possessions, and satisfaction. There is no end to the need for protection or security for fragile creatures and, as it is often said, human needs may be limited and satiable but human wants, especially for things like security, power, longevity, approval, and status are commonly indefinite or insatiable. Therefore, the pursuit of instrumental control over events, including the many kinds of human suffering, tends to be unending and to squeeze out other kinds of goals in living going forward, our stark human finitude be damned.

Cognitive-Behavioral Therapy

As mentioned earlier, some years ago Jerome Frank (1978) argued astutely that the value systems of 20th-century psychotherapies accord "primacy to individual self-fulfillment" in a way that "can easily become a source of misery in itself" (p. 6). I think it is the disguised ideology of most of these therapies, giving a predominant place to individualism and instrumentalism in some form, that leads them to emphasize autonomous self-direction and instrumental control over events in a way that can indeed cause misery in itself, including by failing to take the measure of inescapable human suffering.

There may be as many different extant therapies in relatively affluent societies today than there are dandelions in my front yard every spring. But consider, for example one of the most common approaches to relieving suffering through psychotherapy, namely cognitive-behavioral therapy (CBT), which has many variants. As Dobson and Dozois (2009) describe it, "CBTs share three fundamental propositions: 1) Cognitive activity affects behavior. 2) Cognitive activity may be monitored and altered. 3) Behavior change may be effected through cognitive change" (p. 4). Alan Kazdin (1978), a prominent psychotherapy researcher and theorist, clarified the instrumental cast of CBT: "The term 'cognitive-behavior modification' encompasses treatments that attempt to change overt behavior by altering thoughts, interpretations, assumptions, and strategies of responding" (p. 337). The basic idea is to pluck out the problematic cognitions and insert health-promoting ones. The main hindrance to successful living in the CBT view is "irrational" or mistaken beliefs that induce painful emotions and maladaptive behavior. Successful therapy severs this connection between attitude and circumstance. "The principal goal of cognitive therapy is to replace the client's presumed distorted appraisals of life events with more realistic and adaptive appraisals" (Dobson & Dozois, 2009, p. 14). This is classic instrumentalism with disposable means toward subjectively preferable ends (Fowers, 2005).

To be sure, adopting this view of things often helps question and counteract common cultural values that indeed contribute to real and unnecessary miseries, such as neurotic fears, excessive guilt, and crippling dependency on the approval of others. Nevertheless, such an approach to healing and a good life is noticeably limited. For the most part, CBT therapies merely take a negative tack. They mainly recommend *not* premising one's sense of self-worth on worldly success or the opinions of others. If CBT theorists are pressed, the most they typically suggest is that more rational thinking will allow people to feel more pleasure and happiness, the only human goods they acknowledge, and to live more "adaptively," without explaining clearly what adaptive means. They say nothing about the affirmative values, purposes, meanings, or connections with others that are central to human fulfillment in many ethical outlooks and traditions. According to the wisdom contained in these ethical viewpoints, traditions, and spiritual perspectives, pleasure is insufficient as the highest human good. Pleasures are entirely too varied and scattered to provide any sort of focus or direction in living (Aristotle, 1999; Fowers, 2005; Fowers et al., 2017). Moreover, some pleasures are quite objectionable, like those enjoyed in grandiosity or dominating others, however much the contemporary world at times may celebrate them as admirable marks of competitive success or achievement or justify them cynically as necessary means to the end of economic development.

In addition, CBT theories obviously adopt the assumptions of the modern moral outlook known as utilitarianism. They do so uncritically without acknowledging these premises or feeling any need to defend them against the many criticisms that have been leveled against this view. For example, the philosopher Bernard Williams (1986, pp. 101–102) has pointed out. Utilitarians portray human beings as engaged in a kind of direct "pursuit of happiness." But this pursuit may be impossible or at least self-defeating. Utilitarianism does involve a kind of morally serious commitment to adhere to the results of calculations concerning both one's own and others' "happiness." That may take self-discipline and, perhaps at times, a bit of self-denial or postponement of self-gratification. But a strong case can be made, Williams argues, that in fact a moral agent does not act from such calculations, but is "identified with his actions as flowing from projects and attitudes which in some cases he takes seriously at the deepest level, as what life is all about." To demand that a person be ready to set these aside if calculations of utility require is "to alienate him in a real sense from his actions and the source of his action in his own convictions." This would really amount to "an attack on his integrity." Few in psychology know anything about this sort of careful analysis in moral philosophy. Patient and therapist alike resonate to a utilitarian outlook and press on ahead uncritically to goals of more "effective" and "rational" living.

Rational emotive behavior therapy (REBT) is "regarded by many as the premiere example of the cognitive-behavioral approach." To reach its main goal, "to maintain a state of emotional health, individuals must constantly monitor and challenge their basic belief systems" (Dobson & Dozois, 2009, pp. 11–12). These methods are designed to help clients "experience a minimum of emotional disturbance" (p. 13). It is fascinating that these theorists seem to treat a person's basic belief systems simply as a tool to be manipulated for the sake of emotional tranquility. However, it is worth taking a closer look at the writings of Albert Ellis (1962, 1977), the originator of rational emotive behavior therapy and one of the most influential psychotherapy theorists of the post-World War II era. Ellis states, rather uncommonly, that "All psychotherapy is, at bottom, a value system" (1973, p. 28). He writes that clients should be encouraged to decide that "it is good for me to live and enjoy myself" and to decide "to strive for more pleasure than pain." Also, he contends that clients are capable of discovering that these values are attractive and correct through evaluations "entirely within the empirical realm" (p. 23).

These remarks may make it seem as if Ellis is simply a straightforward advocate of what he has calls "long-range hedonism" (1973, p. 23), perhaps thereby giving a nod to the fact that maximizing pleasure and tranquility over the long run may periodically require postponement of some satisfactions. Today, most CBT therapies adopt a straightforward, fairly simplistic, and kind of psychological technology. But as a serious clinician Albert Ellis reckoned more profoundly with life's dark side. In his writings, he seems at times to fret about what he terms our "inborn biological tendency" to think irrationally or "magically," leading to self-blame, blame of others, and emotional disturbance (e.g., 1973, p 23). Indeed, it seems as if the struggle against this tendency, rather than simply striving for pleasure, becomes the main business of living! Ellis appreciates the paradoxical stubbornness of human masochism and self-defeat. Moreover, he may be interpreted as proposing a cure for this misery that goes beyond ordinary therapy technique, namely his own recommended philosophical outlook.

This outlook appears to have two distinct elements. One element is a thoroughgoing, explicitly nonreligious *hedonism* that provides the goals for human action conceived in narrowly utilitarian and instrumentalist terms. The second is less obvious but crucial to Ellis's approach. It is a strong emphasis on a kind of *detachment*—a detachment from the lottery of love and fortune that bears some resemblance to traditional philosophical or religious stances toward life, such as the Stoic ideal of freedom from destructive passions in a life lived in accordance with nature, or a Christian view of life lived "in but not of the world." Though far from advocating any sort of transcendental views or values, Ellis seems to appreciate that simple hedonism is insufficient for human beings remorselessly exposed to many disappointments, evils, tragedies, suffering, and death. "Irrational beliefs," after all, are irrational because they make individuals' equanimity or sense of self-worth dependent upon external circumstances, such as achievement, the approval of others, or the absence of frustration or discomfort in their lives. The most basic thing that successful therapy does is *sever this connection* between attitude and circumstance that is deemed by the theory to be unnecessary or rationally indefensible. Indeed, what Ellis calls the truly "elegant" rational-emotive therapy solution to fundamental human dilemmas occurs when people finally arrive at the point where "practically under all conditions for the rest of their lives would not upset themselves about anything" (quoted in Weinrach, 1980, p. 156).

The trouble is, however, that this ideal of detachment and the best kind of life is confusing and questionable. The original Stoic notion of detachment from excessive attachments and destructive passions only made sense in the context of belief in a kind of living, rational cosmic order that afforded a consoling sense of community with the universe and acceptance of one's place in it. But Ellis's version of detachment, unlike such traditional notions of a meaningful cosmic order, does not function to orient persons toward "higher" ethical or religious realities. Could it then mean complete detachment from all cares or feelings of any sort? That could be accomplished equally well by catatonia or suicide. Is it a matter of just pretending to oneself that pleasures do not mean so much or disappointments wound so sharply as they otherwise would? But that would hardly be possible when seeking pleasure and avoiding pain are the only credible goals in living for humans.

No doubt the rational-emotive framework can assist individuals in reconsidering their strategies in living and putting their all too human concerns in some larger perspective. It may, indeed, give REBT therapists and clients tools to identify and alter some neurotic, defensive patterns of living that are only self-defeating in the long run. Moreover, we might say that this therapy theory has taken a serious stab at a kind of wisdom that may be the object of perennial search: how to become and stay involved in life in a nondefensive and meaningful way in spite of its great uncertainty and inevitable pain and disappointments. But REBT's vision of life remains critically vague concerning how to steer some middle path between meaninglessness and harmful naiveté, or perhaps between what Hall (1986) termed "cynicism" and "credulity," in dealing with human suffering. It is not at all clear how detachment can function as a device to meliorate hedonism without transforming its goals. As a matter of fact, this approach seems to bear some resemblance to the attempt—many would consider it seriously inauthentic—to become emotionally involved with a person or committed to some enterprise, but somehow remain invulnerable to pain or despair.

Important recent developments in the CBT world are Acceptance and Commitment Therapy (ACT) and Mindfulness-Based Cognitive Behavioral Therapy (Hayes, Pistorello, & Levin, 2012; Segal, Williams, & Teasdale, 2004). Their differences notwithstanding, both these approaches share a focus on mindfulness and meditation. These therapies are less coarsely instrumental than traditional CBT. They focus less on simply substituting one cognition with another. Instead, they seek to help clients to "relate" differently to their cognitions and emotions.

For example, "acceptance" in ACT refers to accepting distress, or difficult situations. In this view, we suffer often because we tend to see our situation as simply unbearable. We may attempt to change the situation by avoiding it or by directly changing the frequency or form of our thoughts about it. But some circumstances cannot be easily altered or altered at all and respect for the intensity of human pain and painful thoughts means acknowledging how terribly difficult changing them can be. A key ACT insight is that, however difficult our inner experience, it will inevitably change in time. In this view, "pain is taken to be a part of life, not a foreign entity to be gotten rid of" (Hayes et al., 2012, p. 985). ACT's core principle is to accept one's situation and one's reactions to it in order to clear the way for taking appropriate action.

"Commitment" in ACT refers to taking such action regardless of the thoughts that accompany the difficulty. Actions should be based on one's chosen values and be inherently rewarding for the individual. The ultimate goal of ACT is "psychological flexibility . . . defined as contacting the present moment as a conscious human being, fully and without defense . . . and persisting or changing behavior in the service of chosen values" (Hayes et al., 2012, p. 985).

ACT therapy somewhat softens a purely instrumental approach to emotional pain and distress. It seems to incorporate some elements of Buddhist Vipassana meditation and other contemplative traditions in which, "one attends to whatever one is experiencing—thoughts, feelings . . . bodily sensations—without selection or judgment and cultivates a keen awareness of the impermanent nature of all experience" (Rubin, 1997, p. 90). Thus, ACT seeks to offer an alternative to suffering by assisting afflicted individuals in coming to grips with their pain and responding to it in creative ways.

In the end, however, not really. Contemplative traditions are underpinned by significantly different worldviews than ACT and other cognitive therapies. A close look suggests that ACT, also, is underpinned by a tacit ideology of liberal individualism and remains significantly colored by modern individualism and instrumentalism. For example, ACT is fully committed to the individualistic notion that values are "freely chosen" and "deeply held" (Hayes et al., 2012, p. 988), based strictly on subjective criteria. This lands us squarely in the middle of the paradox discussed in chapter 3. We (1) insist on an uncompromising stress on autonomy and self-interest, a kind of moral relativism that makes all ideals of the good life strictly a matter of individual preference or choice. But at the same time we (2) nevertheless promote serious commitment to a way of life incorporating human rights and dignity that we consider morally superior or *good in itself*. Our society's paramount ethical ideal of "autonomy" or "freedom" asserts both of these ideas at the same time in a confused manner.

Perhaps ACT therapy endorses "acceptance" of pain and suffering mainly instrumentally because if endured, one can return to ordinary satisfactions and enjoyments. But these are weak medicine for life's significant losses, hurts, or despair. Or perhaps ACT's notion of acceptance reflects a kind of existentialist affirmation of one's chosen meanings in the face of life's supposed meaninglessness. But we will see in the next section that this kind of existentialism doesn't hold up very well, either.

Existentialism and Existential Psychotherapy

The existential philosophy of Jean-Paul Sartre (1956) that emerged shortly after World War II represents, in part, a distinctive approach to understanding and coping with human suffering that has since exerted a great deal of influence in academic circles, society at large, and the field of psychology.

There are a number of schools of thought that describe themselves as some form of existentialism, including what is often termed the religious existentialism of Gabriel Marcel (2013) and Karl Jaspers (1986) and the decidedly secular or nonreligious kind of existentialism that has been prominent in popular culture and influential in the arenas of counseling and psychotherapy.

Rollo May and Irwin Yalom (1989) describe existential psychotherapy as providing the key to coping with the challenges and ambiguities of life in a post-traditional world. This view clarifies what it really means to gain personal integrity as opposed to hapless conformity and a sense of direction as opposed to being overmastered by the whims of others. Its key principles are to (1) face the inevitability of death, (2) acknowledge that our cultural and moral values are ultimately groundless and relative, (3) accept the fact of life's meaninglessness in an indifferent universe, and (4) accept the radical responsibility of choosing the ideals and projects that define one's life. "Authenticity" means embracing our freedom and responsibility in this way. This action alone is thought to represent a truly effective antidote for the complacent drifting and timid conformism of everyday life or the internalized fears and guilt trips of therapy patients.[2]

There is no doubt that existentialism has helped many people question the determinism and conformity in modern life that undermine human freedom, personal responsibility, and one's ability to lead a more authentic life. However, existentialism incurs serious difficulties that undermine its ability to sustain courage, vitality, and a sense of direction or purpose in the face of human limitations and suffering. It has been pointed out, for example (Guignon & Pereboom, 1995; Richardson, Fowers, & Guignon, 1999), that Sartre's (1956) philosophy provides no reason whatsoever to justify *why* we should exercise what he calls our "ontological freedom" or "terrible freedom" rather than opt for a life of short-term hedonism, outright sadism, or drug-induced stupor. Similarly, May and Yalom's (1989) central idea of "commitment" for its own sake would seem to treat all ethical ideals and ends in living as mere means to pregiven, purely arbitrary, and presumably dispensable ends. (Thus, it actually amounts to a kind of instrumentalism.) This erodes commitment and undercuts its benefits. If we choose a commitment, can we not unchoose it just as easily? This kind of unbounded freedom seems to enable us to opt out of marital commitments, communal obligations, and even parental responsibilities if and when we change our minds, even on a mere whim.[3]

Undoubtedly, existentialism makes a contribution by encouraging us to face the kinds of human suffering, tragedy, and threats of meaninglessness that so much of modern culture and psychology tend to sweep under the rug. It provides an illuminating critique of aspects of modern life and makes a contribution to clarifying what Taylor argues is a paramount modern virtue or ethical ideal, namely personal authenticity.

However, existentialism's analysis of the human situation seems less than fully authentic. Choice for its own sake, like commitment for its own sake, is reduced to triviality.

One of the key elements of human suffering is that it undermines our ability to maintain our most cherished ideals, relationships, and projects. In the face of suffering, we yearn for and need some ways to share our experiences of vulnerability, pain, and loss. This can take many forms, such as receiving emotional support from loved ones, giving others emotional support, service to others, religious faith, or commitment to projects that are much larger than we are as individuals. A Swedish proverb reminds us that shared suffering is halved and shared joy is doubled. But the existential view leaves each of us stranded in a brave, but isolated and unsustainable freedom.

Existentialism appears designed to honestly embrace a sense of strict meaninglessness while at the same time escaping or at least considerably softening its blow.[4] However, it seems unlikely to have found a way to have cake and eat it, too. If pushed, it either would have to admit that its own recommended way of life is really not worth living at all, or it would have to articulate what is truly worthwhile about it, thereby appealing to some sort of meaning, purpose, or value that amounts to something more than just a product of raw existential choice.

Positive Psychology

The sunny, influential contemporary movement of "positive psychology" places an admirable emphasis on cultivating human strengths and flourishing. It highlights many ways to improve life and help people overcome various kinds of pain and difficulty.[5] But it lacks even REBT's and existentialism's effort to get serious about the dark side of human existence. Its unrelenting focus on the positive leaves positive psychology wrong-footed when it is confronted by serious instances of human pain, loss, and spiritual emptiness. It fails to come to grips with the fact that vulnerability and suffering are part of the warp and woof of our existence Just to illustrate this, it is interesting to note several terms that do not even appear in the index of Chris Peterson and Martin Seligman's (2004) major positive psychology treatise, *Character Strengths and Virtues*. Those terms are loss, hurt, misery, pain, grief, and suffering. The experiences they refer to are absent or underemphasized in the positive psychology literature generally even though they are inescapable aspects of every human life.

Sam Binkley (2011, 2014) provides an especially illuminating account of the foibles of positive psychology. His analysis makes it clear that positive psychology thoroughly decontextualizes individuals from culture and tradition and radically instrumentalizes its view of human action in the world. In other words, it raises individualism and instrumentalism to a fever pitch!

Binkley (2011, p. 377) writes that a "singularly interdisciplinary . . . new discourse on happiness," whose leading edge is positive psychology, has emerged in the last 20 years or so. Binkley notes the "preoccupation of modern societies with the intentional production of human happiness has long been demeaned by some in the social science literature as a dangerous byproduct of . . . societal modernization . . . and . . . capitalist development," with "emotional life . . . deployed as the errand boy of the culture and economy," as in "C. Wright Mills's . . . uniquely unflattering characterization of the over-administered individual as a 'cheerful robot.'" Cultural conservatives such as Daniel Bell "have long lamented the hedonistic demise of civic character brought on by rising rates of consumption." Liberal critics like Barbara Ehrenreich, he writes, link the "compulsory optimism implicit within happiness discourse to a neoconservative political agenda with thinly veiled corporate aims" resulting in . . . Bush-era foibles such as "Enron [and] the invasion of Iraq." Other critics are concerned less with a "threatened sociality" and more with a "truncated subjectivity," one that "fundamentally elides psychological depth and human significance." For example, he notes that Eric Wilson (2009) in a book entitled *Against Happiness: In Praise of Melancholy* acclaims the kind of "melancholia" that "serves as the . . . aesthetic and creative crucible of a romantic subjectivity."

Many of these critics lament our society's tendency to endorse "happiness," understood in terms of a shallow consumerism and materialism, as the best kind of life. Surely they are on to something important. But a closer look suggests that they offer very little in the way of a genuine alternative to some form of liberal individualism (Sandel, 1996) or liberal voluntarism (Deneen, 2018). They seem to endorse liberating individuals from arbitrary authority or domination by others, including social conformity and submissiveness, but refrain from articulating any understanding of the good for humans that would make it possible to evaluate the worth of the patterns or the kinds of personal or social living we might plump for on any basis other than the sheer fact that they are preferred or chosen. And indeed, positive psychology falls right in line with this approach. Binkley (2011) analyzes how a variety of popular positive psychology books specifically instruct readers in the "strategic pursuit of personal satisfaction." He illustrates how in several of these texts other people, even one's spouse, "[enter] into the happiness equation, not as another person, an emotional interlocutor, friend or object of desire or aggressions, but as an instrument for the maximization of one's emotional happiness" (p. 390). In order to accomplish these aims, Binkley (2011) pungently describes how positive psychology assembles a grab bag of techniques from counseling and clinical psychology to guide individuals in altering their cognitive outlooks so they view themselves and their situation in a more favorable light. Anything that looks at all promising will do but, of course, techniques whose effectiveness has been empirically confirmed would be ideal. Their application results, he writes, in an "emotional flush" that they expect "will move clients to perform on such a positive level as to confirm to this initial positive view" (p. 375).

I suspect Binkley finds value in these liberal humanist critiques but realizes there is no simple or obvious way to formulate an attractive alternative to them. In any case, he elects to dig deeper and offer a more penetrating diagnosis of the problem by interpreting positive psychology as "a program of neoliberal governmentality" (2011, p. 377). Drawing on postmodern or poststructuralist thinkers like Foucault (1980) and Rose (1999), he employs a "governmentality" perspective according to which "systems of power" or "regimes of truth" (Foucault, 1980) govern particular cultural discourses and forms of life. Sets of discursive, productive rules operate behind the backs of social actors and shape their activities, reflections, and speech. They take them for granted and think in their terms.

Binkley (2011, 2014) draws on the ideas of Foucault (1980, 2008), also elaborated by others (e.g., Harvey, 2005; Rose, 1999; Sugarman, 2015), which richly describe a newly emergent "neoliberal" system of power in the modern West, and spreading elsewhere. According to the theoretical psychologist Jeff Sugarman (2015, p. 104), some of its key features are

> a radically free market in which competition is maximized, free trade achieved through economic deregulation, privatization of public assets, vastly diminished state responsibility over areas of social welfare, the corporatization of human services, and monetary and social policies congenial to corporations and disregardful of the consequences

such as growing inequality, "rapid depletion of resources, irreparable damage to the biosphere, destruction of cultures, and erosion of liberal democratic institutions."

To the extent that liberal individualism represents our dominant social and political outlook, it is quite understandable how neoliberal attitudes and practices could come to pass. Liberal individualism rather paradoxically combines (1) a morally serious stress on universal human rights and dignity (its own vision of the right and good kind of life) with (2) the insistence that all notions of the human good must be left to the choice or preference of particular individuals or communities (in order to bar any sort of arbitrary authority), assuming only that they don't interfere with the similar choice of other persons or communities. In chapter 3, following writers like Selznick (1992) and Sandel (1996), it was argued that this radical privatizing of notions of the good life seems bound to gradually undermine the commitment to respect human rights and dignity, which is liberal individualism's own ideal of the good life or good society, and according to the chilling account of Mirowski (2018) that is exactly what has taken place in the increasingly influential neoliberal view over recent decades.

Several theoretical psychologists have argued that these neoliberal trends have significant implications for the field of psychology. Sugarman (2013) argues persuasively that even though psychologists are "underequipped . . . to speak of sociopolitical and economic matters," we have no choice but to delve into them. Selfhood, action, and aims in living "take their form from the kinds of relations in which human beings are immersed," and . . . politics—the organized influence and control of others, or what Foucault (2008) referred to as governmentality, is a constitutive feature of both collective and individual psychological life. They "govern the soul" (Rose, 1999). Sugarman (2015, p. 103) writes that "neoliberalism is reformulating personhood, psychological life, moral and ethical responsibility, and what it means to have selfhood and identity." Martin and McLellan (2013) astutely identify an "enterprise culture" that mandates, almost to the exclusion of any others, "personal attributes" of "initiative, self-reliance, self-mastery, and risk-taking," which amount essentially to the "entrepreneurial activity of individuals" (Sugarman, 2015, p. 6).

The urgency of investigating this matter may be illustrated by a much-discussed *New Republic* article by William Deresiewicz a few years ago entitled "Don't Send Your Kid to the Ivy League" (Deresiewicz, 2014a) and in his recent book *Excellent Sheep* (Deresiewicz, 2014b) Deresiewicz describes how a great many students in elite colleges are terrified of not being highly successful, leading to a "violent aversion to risk," loss of any passion for ideas, and giving no attention to developing skills in critical thinking or questioning assumptions. They are abetted in this by a curriculum that trains them "in the analytic and rhetorical skills that are necessary for success in business and the professions. Everything is technocratic—the development of expertise—and everything is ultimately justified in technocratic terms." Of course, there are exceptions. But, he contends, "beneath the façade of seamless well-adjustment . . . what you find often are toxic levels of fear, anxiety, and depression, of emptiness and aimlessness and isolation." He notes that a large-scale survey of college freshmen recently found that self-reports of emotional well-being have fallen to their lowest level in the study's 25-year history.[6]

Binkley (2011) shows how positive psychology reinforces neoliberal trends. It charts a path down which individuals can break from "docility of social dependency . . . resignation . . . [and] reluctance to act on one's own" to achieve "neoliberal subjectivity . . . or freedom" (p. 385). His analysis brings to light how positive psychology takes us beyond a critique of how social modernization seduces or coerces individuals into shallow kinds of "happiness" and illuminates the "prescriptive, reflexive and instrumental dimensions" of positive psychology "whereby subjects are induced to work on themselves and their emotional states as open-ended problems of self-government." They do so through learning specific practices for the "enactment of subjectivities adequate to the ends of governmental strategies that span the public and the private" realms. Individuals now do much of the dirty work themselves of maintaining the neoliberal regime. Nice work if you can get it!

The whole point of this approach is to free individuals from unwanted, enterprise-hampering social and psychological dependencies of many kinds so that they can function as untrammeled, endlessly entrepreneurial selves. Yet this program for freedom and fulfillment, according to Binkley (2011), requires that individuals slavishly accept a phony "scientific" authority— namely positive psychology—without question or debate, giving them no recourse except to blame themselves and just keep on trying if doubts arise or things do not seem to be working out as one had hoped. No matter what is said about putting power and efficacy in individuals' own hands and freeing them from dependency on community, tradition, or even more traditional psychotherapies, they are encouraged throughout to depend uncritically on positive psychology experts for knowledge, wisdom, coaching, and guidance that cannot be challenged!

It is hard to exaggerate the paradoxical, ironic, hubristic, and somewhat nightmarish character of positive psychology's approach. Binkley's (2011, 2013) writings bring a lot of that to light and expose some of the depths of the problem, including, I would add, the sad fact that the barren social landscape projected by positive psychology is a place where little of ubiquitous human suffering can be seen and little can be done to address it. The only real options for addressing suffering in positive psychology are to ignore it or reframe the problem in positive terms. This might be good advice for minor bouts of depression or small disappointments, but something more or different is needed when we lose loved ones, come to recognize that we have committed a serious transgression, face our mortality, or are coming to terms with a devastating natural disaster.

Illuminating as it is, however, we do not require the full apparatus of a Foucauldian governmental view to capture the ways in which individuals can remain blind to the forces and values that unawares drive their living and choices. We don't have to buy it completely to capture the ways individuals sell out much of their freedom and responsibility in order to fit it or belong to wider communities or societies that promise them security and readily obtainable rewards and threaten them with disapproval or isolation if they do not pursue the right goals. Critical psychologists (e.g., Cushman, 1990; Richardson et al., 1999; Slife, Smith, & Burchfield, 2003) have argued that modern psychotherapy theory and practice engage in at least some of this kind of deception. Typically, they present their theories and practices as value-free or value-neutral while endorsing and propagating disguised ideologies that excuse them from challenging important aspects of the cultural status quo. One hopes the governmental perspective is not the last word on how this comes about because in fact this approach has serious difficulties.

The case has been made (Bishop, 2007; Guignon, 1991; Richardson et al., 1999; Taylor, 1985c) that every critique like Foucault's or Binkley's always *presupposes* some working notion of the human good. The flaws they detect only count as inadequate if critiquing them exposes ways they fall sort of *some* ideal of a more honest, decent, authentic, or meaningful kind of life. The critique only counts or means something if, in part, it represents a starting point for discerning something better. Surely that is why capable critics like Binkley (2011, 2014) do the work they do. They realize they have to dig deeper to expose the subtle ways that individuals "sell out" to a shallow social order and have to take account of the wider cultural patterns and practices that would have to be transformed if something more authentic were to arise. For example, deeper and wiser individuals might require a more modest and collaborative way of life that would in turn foster deeper and wiser individuals.

However, Binkley's critique of the program of neoliberal governmentality, illuminating in some ways, remains entirely silent on the question of the human good. Thus it remains true to its Foucauldian premises. In Foucault's (1980) view, anything that we might call a "truth" about the good or right life is simply an "effect" of the rules or power relations that constitute particular discourses or forms of life, about which there simply is no overall truth or falsity. Here, as in many postmodern or social constructionist approaches, the human self seems to be sharply divided between (1) an embedded, ultimately hapless social actor, a mere creature of the current "regime of truth," and (2) a creative and insightful social theorist who takes intelligent note of all this from a disengaged and far distant vantage point (Richardson et al., 1999, pp. 188–195). This view is quite paradoxical and seems in the end implausible. Discerning and insightful social theorists, morally motivated in part, must be capable of helping to foster a better world, or else they have to give up any claim that their analysis of the social realm is true or valid.

It is interesting to note how both typically modern and would-be postmodern viewpoints of this sort share certain basic features. Both impose a sharp gulf between persons and their world and between fact and value.

They seem to represent different versions of what Nagel (1987) famously termed a "view from nowhere." (For this reason, Selznick (1992) shrewdly characterizes much postmodern thought as the "wayward child of modernism," carrying its logic to extremes rather than presenting a genuine alternative.) Both become entangled in paradoxes that portray human agents as both determined and free in a contradictory fashion. And both fail to reveal any path from their considerable detachment as social scientists or theorists to constructive cultural revision. Mainstream social science tends to be limited to providing knowledge that might be useful to social actors in a narrowly *instrumental* way. Postmodern thinkers take things a step further and invite readers to join them in a kind of austere wisdom of detachment as , an end in itself.[7] From such a detached point of view, it is very difficult to recognize, empathize with, come to terms with, or find meaning in human suffering other than simply eliminating it instrumentally through some kind of medical or technological means.

Antihumanism

Charles Taylor (2007) identifies an important stream in the culture of the modern West, namely antihumanism, which exemplifies, in part, a distinctive attempt to squarely face human suffering. This view is usually associated with the philosophy of Friedrich Nietzsche (1967). Typically, only a fairly small number of intellectuals or well-read individuals explicitly espouse an antihumanist outlook. But it has influenced many thinkers and theorists for whom some version seems like the only alternative to sappy modern optimism or a naive belief in human progress. This approach shares modern secular humanism's rejection of any sort of good beyond human life, especially any notion of God or transcendence. But it also disparages what Taylor calls humanism's "affirmation of ordinary life," which it sees as confining, stifling, and embracing of a kind of anti-elitism or rejection of excellence that undermines the possibility of any sort of enhanced life. In this view, humanism's animus against hierarchy, aggression, and even some forms of violence is a "culpable weakness." Further, its "belief in untroubled happiness" is not only a "childish illusion, but involves a truncation of human nature" (Taylor, 2007, p. 635). Instead of voiding life of its heroic dimension, we should find something to celebrate in aggression and in "the urge to fight, dominate, even inflict suffering" (p. 634), which Nietzsche famously saw as possible expressions of a "will to power." Humanism, however, "tends to hide from itself how great the conflict is between the different things we value" and "artificially removes the tragedy, the wrenching choices between incompatibles, the dilemmas, which are inseparable from human life" (p. 635).

A version of antihumanism is reflected in Michel Foucault's (1980) insistence that *all* conceptions of the good life, including modern liberal ideals of universal and equal respect, are ultimately arbitrary "regimes of truth," imposed orders of shaping or domination that historically succeed one another but do not represent any sort of "progress." Another classic expression of antihumanism is Nietzsche's argument that Judaism, Christianity, and modern liberal ideals all reflect a kind of "slave morality" because they excuse weaker or lesser souls for their failure to excel and create, and moralistically, inauthentically, demand an unearned esteem and protection from noble or powerful others in spite of their own deficiencies.

Perhaps neo-Nietzschean or antihumanist views have some power to help expose modern hypocrisies, such as shallow conformism that lays claim to moral superiority or the kind of political correctness that pillories all sorts of discriminations and dominations while masking its own judgmental and controlling sort of power trip. Perhaps, like Aldous Huxley's *Brave New World*, they shed light on the sort of modern "dystopia in which the goals of pleasure and stability have crowded out every other human good, burying discontent under antidepressants, genetic engineering, and virtual-reality escapades" (Douthat, 2013). Perhaps they hint at the sense of courage, adventure, and genuine risk-taking we often feel are missing in our world. But surely antihumanism is at risk here of throwing out the baby with the bath water. Is it really wise to reject core liberal values of equal dignity and moral equality (not equality of ability or achievement) just because some in modern times elect to make a fetish of their freedom, succumb to narcissism, or emphasize protecting their rights to the neglect of all other ethical concerns? At its best, it can take immense character and skill to enact our liberal credo of respect and restraint, in both public and private life, to the potential benefit of all. It is hard to see how any ethically serious soul could really make their peace with the violence and cruelty that ensue in the absence of those basic liberal values or some facsimile of them. It might make more sense to address the insufficiencies of that hard-won credo, for which much blood, sweat, and tears have been shed, and allow facing human suffering to guide us toward a more mature and credible version of the human story or struggle. There is no guarantee that path will not end up in dejection or despair. But to close off the inquiry at the outset without even trying seems uncourageous and decidedly inauthentic.

Notes

1. I find Schumaker's analysis of these issues quite illuminating. But it should be noted that for the most part he does not even discuss the problem of how we might fashion anything like shared "cultural coping strategies" in a modern, pluralistic,

individualistic, society where a great many citizens are either close-minded and dogmatic about their moral or religious beliefs or else tend to be skeptical, even cynical, about the possibility of finding shared meanings or ethical ideals with which to meet pain, loss, and moral confusion.

2. A student of mine once told me the story of her best friend in therapy in New York whose therapist suggested to her from time to time, when she became especially depressed, to remember, "Life is nothing but a spinach salad." Perhaps we need a new raft of children's books written by existentialists to convey this message to young children before they are seduced into taking any cultural and moral values seriously as anything other than discardable objects of personal choice!

3. Of course, proponents of existentialism or existential psychotherapy do not intend to undermine mature ethical commitments or responsibilities. Rather, their view, in the end, seems to assume some version of conventional liberal individualism they would never unchoose, one that endorses "freedom from" arbitrary authority and any number of oppressive or benumbing influences, has little to say about any sort of compelling "freedom for" beyond freedom itself, and just implausibly assumes that things will somehow work out satisfactorily on their own.

4. The parallel with REBT discussed earlier is remarkable. Both seem to couple a hard-nosed sense of being fairly isolated individuals in an impersonal society and indifferent cosmos with an exuberant, one might say "comic," sense of almost unlimited possibilities for freedom and happiness.

5. A thorough review and critique of positive psychology by a number of theoretical psychologists can be found in the articles in a special issue of the journal *Theory & Psychology*, 2008, volume 18.

6. It has been pointed out that many university students do not resemble their elite peers in this regard, especially first-generation students and those from impoverished and sometimes war torn countries. They often are quite inner-directed, deeply committed to social justice, and dedicated to serving their communities. But one wonders if life in a narrowly technocratic, individualistic, intensely competitive society will not undermine their own and their progeny's best values over time. "Exceptional sheep" may represent much of the future unless we do something about it.

7. The irony in all this is that social scientists come up with very little or nothing in term of well-developed, predictive theory on the natural science model (Bernstein, 1976; Root, 1993; Taylor, 1985a) while many postmodernists are passionate liberals who, mistakenly, feel that Foucault's notion of our being "dominated" by one or another system of power gives them a tool for liberating individuals from discrimination and oppression—when in fact , in the Foucauldian view, they are not fostering "freedom" but enacting their star-crossed role in just another "regime of truth." If this chapter's analysis is correct, both are commonly committed liberal individualists who obscure the role their (quite sincere) ethical commitments play in their theorizing or research.

References

Aristotle. (1999). *Nichomachean ethics* (M. Ostwald, Trans.). Upper Saddle River, NJ: Prentice Hall.

Bernstein, R. J. (1976). *The restructuring of social and political theory*. Philadelphia: University of Pennsylvania Press.

Binkley, S. (2011). Happiness, positive psychology and the program of neoliberal governmentality. *Subjectivity, 4*, 371–394. http://doi.org/10.1057/sub.2011.16

Binkley, S. (2013). *Happiness as enterprise: An essay on neoliberal life*. Albany: State University of New York Press.

Binkley, S. (2014). Happiness as enterprise: An essay on neoliberal life. Suny Press.

Bishop, R. C. (2007). *The philosophy of the social sciences: An introduction*. New York: Continuum.

Brown, W. (2003). Neo-liberalism and the end of liberal democracy. *Theory & Event, 7*. Retrieved from http://muse.jhu.edu.ezproxy.lib.utexas.edu/

Cushman, P. (1990). Why the self is empty. *American Psychologist, 45*, 599–611.

Davies, B., & Bansel, P. (2007). Neoliberalism and education. *International Journal of Qualitative Studies in Education, 20*, 247–259. https://doi.org/10.1080/09518390701281751

Deneen, P. (2018). *Why liberalism failed*. New Haven, CT: Yale University Press

Deresiewicz, W. (2014a, July). Don't send your kid to the Ivy League. *The New Republic*. Retrieved from https://newrepublic.com/article/118747/ivy-league-schools-are-overrated-send-your-kids-elsewhere.

Deresiewicz, W. (2014b). *Excellent sheep: The miseducation of the American elite*. New York: The Free Press.

Dobson, K., & Dozois, D. (2009). Historical and philosophical bases of the cognitive-behavioral therapies. In K. Dobson (Ed.), *Handbook of cognitive-behavioral therapies* (3rd ed., pp. 3–38). New York: Guilford Press.

Douthat, R. (2013, November 23). Puddleglum and the savage. *The New York Times*.

Ellis, A. (1962). *Reason and emotion in psychotherapy*. New York: Lyle Stuart.

Ellis, A. (1973). *Humanistic psychotherapy*. New York: McGraw-Hill.

Ellis, A. (1977). The basic clinical theory of rational-emotive psychotherapy. In A. Ellis & R. Grieger (Eds.), *Handbook of rational-emotive psychotherapy*. New York: Springer.

Foucault, M. (1980). *Power/knowledge: Selected interviews and other writings* (C. Gordon, Ed.). New York: Pantheon.

Foucault, M. (2008). *The birth of biopolitics: Lectures at the Collège de France 1978–979*. Basingstoke: Palgrave Macmillan. https://doi.org/10.1057/9780230594180

Fowers, B. (2005). *Virtue ethics and psychology: Pursuing excellence in ordinary practices*. Washington, DC: APA Press Books.

Fowers, B., Richardson, F., & Slife, B. (2017). *Frailty, suffering, and vice: Flourishing in the face of human limitations*. Washington, DC: American Psychological Association Press Books.

Frank, J. (1978). *Psychotherapy and the human predicament*. New York: Schocken.

Guignon, C. (1991). Pragmatism or hermeneutics? Epistemology after foundationalism. In D. Hiley, J. Bohman, & R. Schusterman (Eds.), *The interpretive turn* (pp. 81–101). Ithaca: Cornell University Press.

Guignon, C., & Pereboom, D. (1995). *Existentialism: Basic writings*. Indianapolis, IN: Hackett.

Hall, D. (1986). *God and human suffering: An exercise in the theology of the cross.* Minneapolis, MN: Augsburg Publishing House.

Harvey, D. (2005). *A brief history of neoliberalism.* New York: Oxford University Press.

Hayes, S., Pistorello, J., & Levin, M. (2012). Acceptance and commitment therapy as a unified model of behavior change. *The Counseling Psychologist, 40*, 976–1002. http://doi.org/10.117/0011000012460386

Held, D. (1980). *Introduction to critical theory.* Berkeley, CA: University of California Press.

Jaspers, K. (1971). *Philosophy of existence.* (R. Graban, Trans.). Philadelphia, PA: University of Pennsylvania Press.

Jaspers, K. (1986). *Basic writings* (E. Ehrlich, L. Ehrlich, & G. Pepper, Eds.). Athens, OH: Ohio University Press.

Kazdin, A. (1978). *History of behavior modification: Experimental foundations of contemporary research.* Baltimore: University Park Press.

Marcel, G. (2013). *Tragic wisdom and beyond.* (S. Jolin and P McCormick, Trans.). Evanston: Northwestern University Press, 1973.

Marcel, G. (2017). *The mystery of being.* New York: Andesite Press.

Martin, J., & McLellan, A. (2013). *The education of selves: How psychology transformed students.* New York: Oxford University Press. http://doi.org/10.1093/acprof:oso/9780199913671.001.0001

May, R., & Yalom, I. (1989). Existential psychotherapy. In R. Corsini & D. Wedding (Eds.), *Current psychotherapies.* Itasca, IL: Peacock.

McCarthy, T. (1978). *The critical theory of Jürgen Habermas.* Cambridge, MA: MIT Press.

McGruder, J. H. (1999). *Madness in Zanzibar: "Schizophrenia" in three families in the "developing" world.* ProQuest, UMI Dissertations Publishing.

Mirowski, P. (2018). Neoliberalism: The movement that dare not speak its name. *American Affairs,* II, #1.

Nagel, T. (1987). *The view from nowhere.* London: Oxford University Press.

Nietzsche, F. (1967). *The will to power.* New York: Random House.

Peterson, C., & Seligman, M. (2004). *Character strengths and virtues: A handbook and classification.* Washington, DC: American Psychological Association.

Richardson, F., Fowers, B., & Guignon, C. (1999). *Re-envisioning psychology: Moral dimensions of theory and practice.* San Francisco, CA: Jossey-Bass.

Rieff, P. (1966). *The triumph of the therapeutic.* New York: Harper.

Root, Michael. (1993). *Philosophy of Social Science.* Oxford, UK: Blackwell.

Rose, N. (1999). *Governing the soul: The shaping of the private self* (2nd ed.). London: Free Association Books.

Rubin, J. (1997). Psychoanalysis is Self-Centered. In C. Spezzano & G. Garguilo (eds.) *Soul on the couch: Spirituality, religion, and morality in contemporary psychoanalysis* (pp. 76–106). Hillsdale, NJ: Analytic Press.

Sandel, M. (1996). *Democracy's discontent: America in search of a public philosophy.* Cambridge, MA: Belknap/Harvard.

Sartre, J. (1956). *Being and nothingness.* New York: Philosophical Library.

Schumaker, J. (2001). *The age of insanity: Modernity and mental health*. Westport, CT: Praeger.

Schwartz, B. (2004). *The paradox of choice: Why more is less*. New York: ECCO.

Segal, Z., Teasdale, J., & Williams, J. (2004). Mindfulness-based cognitive therapy: Theoretical rationale and empirical status. In S. C. Hayes, V. M. Follette, & M. M. Linehan (Eds.), *Mindfulness and acceptance: Expanding the cognitive-behavioral tradition* (pp. 45–65). Guilford Press.

Selznick, P. (1992). *The moral commonwealth*. Berkeley, CA: University of California Press.

Slife, B., Smith, A., & Burchfield, C. (2003). Psychotherapists as crypto-missionaries: An exemplar on the crossroads of history, theory, and philosophy. In D. Hill & M. Krall (Eds.), *About psychology: At the crossroads of history, theory, and philosophy* (pp. 55–72). Albany, NY: SUNY Press.

Sugarman, J. (2013, October). Neoliberalism and the ethics of psychology. *Paper presented at the psychology and the other conference*. Cambridge, MA.

Sugarman, J. (2015). Neoliberalism and psychological ethics. *Journal of Theoretical and Philosophical Psychology, 35*, 103–116.

Taylor, C. (1985a). *Philosophy and the human sciences: Philosophical papers* (Vol. 2). Cambridge: Cambridge University Press.

Taylor, C. (1989). *Sources of the self*. Cambridge, MA: Harvard University Press.

Taylor, C. (2007). *A secular age*. Cambridge, MA: Belknap Press of Harvard University Press.

Watters, E. (2010). *Crazy like us: The globalization of the American psyche*. New York: Free Press.

Weinrach, S. (1980, Spring). Unconventional therapist: Albert Ellis. *The Personnel and Guidance Journal*, 152–159.

Williams, B. (1986). *Ethics and the limits of philosophy*. Cambridge. Mass.: Harvard.

Wilson, E. (2008). *Against happiness: In praise of melancholy*. New York, NY: Sarah Crichton Books.

Wilson, E. (2009). *Against happiness*. New York: Sarah Chrichton Books.

6   Toward a "New Wisdom of Limits"

In his last writings before his untimely death, Christopher Lasch (1991, 1995) spoke about the "forbidden topic of limits" in recent times and about our pressing need for a "new wisdom of limits," without which genuine democracy cannot be maintained or enhanced. Lasch does not discuss at length, but does touch on in places, human suffering or the tragic side of life. I suggest that such an absence of wisdom of concerning human limits is a major source of psychology's neglect of the vast dimension of human suffering. I will turn to Lasch's penetrating discussion of this matter in a moment. To begin with, however, it is important to gain some insight into just how the epistemology and methods of modern psychology enshrine this absence of any wisdom of limits at the heart of the field's approach to its subject matters.

Empiricism and Descriptivism

Chapter 3 argued that the claims of most social science in the 20th and 21st centuries, psychology included, to be value-neutral or value-free are fairly preposterous (Bishop, 2007; Richardson, Fowers, & Guignon, 1999; Slife, Smith, & Burchfield, 2003). This seems to be the case, even though much of their status and claims to relevance in the academy and wider society depend upon their living up to that ideal. It is the only thing that distinguishes them, many feel, from biased and opinionated preachers, politicians, and benighted ordinary citizens.

On the contrary, Brinkmann (2010) suggests that it would be more appropriate to describe psychology as a "moral science." Part of what Brinkmann has in mind is that social scientists often seem oblivious to the fact that when they select or define a variable such as aggression, self-esteem, self-efficacy, shame, dependency, or a host of others, or when they employ such ideas or principles as psychological well-being, effectiveness, interpersonal conflict, personality integration, and the like,

DOI: 10.4324/9780203731840-7

they are trafficking in an intimate and profound way with cultural meanings and values. Some of these ideas would be puzzling, meaningless, or even contemptible to individuals living in an African village, classical Greece, or the China of Confucius' day. Social scientists and theorists are not standing outside or apart from the stream of history or turbulent human struggles as ideals of strict objectivity or value-freedom imply. Rather they are *immersed* in and are always *participating* seriously in one or another cultural context or tradition. They seek to map or clarify the dynamics of meaningful, goal-oriented human action. And they do this in order to advance human welfare or the human good in some way that makes sense in their social world.

Why, one wonders, would intellectually capable and often socially concerned researchers and theorists adhere fervently to an ideal of value neutrality or stringent objectivity that, taken seriously, renders their ideas and findings strictly irrelevant to the evaluation or conduct of human affairs? Among other shortcomings, embracing this ideal makes it exceptionally difficult to acknowledge the reality of extensive human suffering or investigate its meaning or dynamics.

Many social scientists, including psychologists, would respond in one of two ways to this critique. First, some would reply that experimental and correlational findings in their field yield information about what causes or conditions regularly produce desirable or undesirable social or psychological effects. Knowing this puts us in a position to re-engineer our practices and perhaps even our psyches for the better. Our value-neutrality actually serves human welfare. What's the problem, they might say? Are you *opposed* to advancing human welfare?

The problem is that they plainly view human action in the world and any interventions done on the basis of their findings in narrowly *instrumental* terms, and such instrumentalism incurs enormous difficulties. One difficulty is that instrumentalism, as discussed in Chapter 3, rather than simply contributing to our rational competency, actually leads to what Horkheimer (1947/2013) called an "eclipse of reason." We may be able to uncover some causal relationships among events and enhance our practical control over them. But we have no ability to evaluate the goodness or worth of such enhanced prowess along with its outcomes or achievements. Any higher purposes or intrinsic values they might serve are regarded as purely arbitrary, subjective, or preferential, leaving us with no overriding purpose beyond expanding our power or control to the fullest extent possible in any arbitrarily chosen direction. This robs a purely instrumental view of any ethical validity or moral force. There is no basis for choosing between, say, producing violence-filled video games or building a museum or cathedral. Whatever sells or tickles one's fancy. Psychology's paramount moral purpose of advancing "effectiveness," by itself, is ultimately hollow and potentially degrading.

A second, even more basic, problem with the instrumental approach is ontological in nature. The field of virtue ethics (Fowers, 2005; Guignon, 1993; MacIntyre, 1981; Richardson, 2012) helps clarify this matter. Fowers (2005) makes the notion of "internal" or "constituent" goods as opposed to "external" goods central to his exposition of virtue ethics. External goods such as wealth, power, prestige, or simple pleasures, comforts, and satisfactions, are the separable outcome of some activity, held as possessions by individuals. Generally speaking, any means will do if it produces the desired result. The supply of external goods is usually limited and they are typically objects of competition. Current critiques of a hypercompetitive neoliberalism (Sugarman, 2015) and harsh meritocracy (Chen, 2016) in effect complain about ways of living that make one-sided instrumental activity and the pursuit of external goods the crux of social life. Among other shortcomings, the instrumental view prevents any serious understanding of or cultivation to any notion of a "common good" in social or political life (Sandel, 2020).

Goods internal to practices are qualitatively different, reflect a different kind of purpose, and are found meaningful in a different way than external goods. According to Fowers (2005, p. 65), one can attain "internal goods only by acting in ways that embody those goods." In the sphere of characterful living that exemplifies virtues or moral excellences means are not at all separable from ends but are "experienced as central to *constituting* a particular way of life."[1] In "constituent-end" as opposed to "means-end" social practices, the whole activity, more or less excellent, "is undertaken for the sake of being such and such." As (Guignon, 1993, p. 230) puts it, "I run as a part of being a healthy person, or I help someone for the sake of being a good friend."

In personal or cultural life external goods are always "subsidiary to" and serve chiefly as an "infrastructure" for the pursuit of internal or constituent goods (Fowers, 2005, p. 60). These seem to be presupposed in some form even by those that deny them. They typically assume *some* intrinsic value or constituent good like fairness, some measure of distributive justice, or compassion even though, just as we have found is the case with liberal individualism, there is little place for those values in their picture of the world.

Internal or constituent goods are not subject to competition because when realized they immediately enrich the life of the wider community or anyone who appreciates them. The practices that incorporate such goods, not instrumental activities, are the most basic and important in human life. They make up who we are as selves or human agents and to the extent we can adopt or cultivate them they set our main directions in living. We may, of course, feel envy or animosity toward someone else's excellence or the admiration they elicit from others. But that occurs only because in addition to any appreciation on our part of the constituent goods involved, we also cling to some extent to external goods of power, social status, or prestige as ends in themselves.

Second, a number of other social scientists today would reply differently to the charge that they are crippled by a disingenuous and ultimately self-defeating value-neutrality. They would claim that, in fact, they have met this problem head-on. They do not, they say, reduce human behavior to something narrowly instrumental and less than fully human. Instead, they portray or describe meaningful human action or lived human experience in terms appropriate to their richness and variety rather than seek to explain them via deterministic general laws. Phenomenological approaches to inquiry in psychology (Valle & Halling, 1989) and other social sciences, ethnomethodology (Hammersley, 2018), and a broad array of methods loosely termed "qualitative" rather than "quantitative" or narrowly empirical in nature (Denzin & Lincoln, 1998) incorporate this view. Bernstein (1976) suggests the helpful label "descriptivist" for these strategies. In varied ways, they all partake of the spirit of Clifford Geertz's credo (1973, p. 5): "Believing, with Max Weber, that man is an animal suspended in webs of significance he himself has spun, I take culture to be those webs, and the analysis of it therefore not to be an experimental science in search of law but an interpretive one in search of meaning."

The philosopher Peter Winch (1958, 1977) elucidates the basic principles of a descriptivist approach to inquiry in a more explicit and careful manner than social scientists usually do. He argues that human action is purposive, inherently social, rule-governed activity. Thus, explaining human action means giving an account of why people do the things they do, namely their motives, reasons, and goals, by formulating the intersubjective rules or standards that constitute their particular form of life or what Winch calls a "form of rationality." The elucidation of rule-following behavior, in this view, is different in kind from explaining nature or society via context-independent general laws. Human action is deeply social and consists more in cooperative activities guided by common meanings and shared values than in radically self-interested behavior. Even in a society like ours where many persons think of themselves as self-directed, self-interested individuals who pursue goals of their own choosing, they have to cooperate extensively with the rules and laws of the market and the state to flourish (Wolfe, 1989). Moreover, having an individualistic outlook is commonplace and the goals of success and satisfaction most chase after are ultimately quite similar. We are far less unique than we often like to think we are.

How should we evaluate this approach to understanding human life? Giddens (1976) argues that social inquiry is characterized by a "double hermeneutic." In his view, postpositivist or postempiricist views of scientific inquiry like Kuhn's (1970) acknowledge the first half of this double herme-neutic. They assert that a science's theory and findings are shaped in crucial ways by the investigators' interpretive framework of assumptions, conven-tions, and purposes, something which applies to natural and human science alike. Descriptivist views of social inquiry, as Winch characterizes them, begin to take account of the other half of this double hermeneutic, which may apply only in the social disciplines where the object of study is the *same* sort of reality or activity as the one that carries out the inquiry. They may not take the full measure of the mutually influencing interplay between investi-gator and subject matter. But descriptivist approaches appreciate that char-acteristic human actions and emotions, unlike events in the natural world, are symbolically structured aspects of social reality.

Descriptivist viewpoints give us valuable insights into the inherently social and moral texture of human life. They suggest that human action is not exclu-sively or even mainly instrumental but largely an enactment of varied forms of life or forms of rationality. Baseline social reality consists of cooperative practices and institutions that embody shared understandings of what life is all about. One or another set of intrinsic values, ethical, religious, aesthetic, or political orient instrumental activities and prereflectively shapes our expe-rience and practices long before we begin to deliberate about such matters.

These gains notwithstanding, Bernstein (1976) argues that descriptivist approaches like Winch's seem to founder when it comes to explicating the *normative* dimensions of social theory. In the "investigation of a human society," Winch (1958) writes, "It is not [our] business to advocate any Welt-anschauung. . . . In Wittgenstein's words, 'Philosophy leaves everything as it was.'" The trouble is, just that statement of Winch's is both morally loaded and self-refuting! It contains a plea for positive values of openness to and respect for the variety of forms of life, and necessarily implies a condemna-tion of any Weltanschauung which excludes those values. (Notice how some version of the disguised ideology of liberal individualism is at work here.) Moreover, Winch remarks movingly that

> the concept of learning from which is involved in the study of other cul-tures is closely linked with the concept of wisdom. We are confronted not just with different techniques, but with new possibilities of good and evil, in relation to which [people] may come to terms with life.
>
> (p. 103)

However, Bernstein observes,

> such a "wisdom" is empty unless it also provides some critical basis for evaluating these "new possibilities of good and evil." Certainly we can

recognize that there are forms of life which are dehumanizing and alien-
ating, and we want to understand precisely in what ways they are so. To
insist that philosophy and social theory remain neutral and uncommit-
ted undermines any rational basis for such a critique of society.

(p. 74)

In the descriptivist view, the social scientist seems to remain detached from
the social reality in which he or she is, in fact, historically embedded and thoroughly a part, in a way that creates much epistemological confusion.[2] Also,
she remains strictly neutral and morally disinterested in a way that obfuscates
the practical aims of social inquiry. Descriptivist approaches, like many phenomenological and "qualitative" research methods, seek to describe meaningful human action and experience on their *own* terms. They reject reducing
them to the causal interplay of objective events and forces or the narrowly
instrumental re-engineering of them according to our desires or preferences,
guided only by whatever merely "subjective" meaning we just happen to
attribute to them. However, they fail one of the most important challenges
facing any social science account of human life, namely showing that and
how it sheds some kind of useful, practical, or ethical light on the conduct of
human affairs. Moreover, they fail to clarify how we might distinguish a true
or accurate from a false or distortive account of the meanings at play except
to claim or imply that a truer or more valid account provides a more *objective*
description or portrayal of them. But this claim overlooks the fact that every
description is highly selective and more or less subtly interprets the events or
experiences it depicts in a way that inescapably reflects the biases and values of the interpreter and his or her community. So, descriptivist approaches
struggle to find a credible alternative to (1) an impossible complete objectivity
or (2) an inappropriate or dogmatic moral or political bias in their accounts.

Both empiricist approaches to social inquiry that adopt a narrowly instrumental view of human action and descriptivist viewpoints on inquiry give
pride of place to a distinctively modern emphasis on expanding power and
control. The instrumentalism of the former endorses a sharp distinction
between fact and value and between means and ends. It limits meaningful or rational human action to what Habermas (1973, p. 254) terms "the
purposive-rational application of techniques assured by empirical science."
Besides denuding the richness and variety of human cultural life, it undermines our ability to reason about the goodness or worth of our activities or
to set priorities in a mortal, complicated, and uncertain existence. Among
other difficulties, it offers no approach to coping with human suffering other
than the eradication of such suffering and its causes, one that the previous
chapter argues is impossible, by itself only exacerbates the problem, and can
contribute its own kind of misery to the mix.

Descriptivist approaches pay respect to a degree to a wider array of possible meanings and goals in living, as they show up in varieties of individual experiences or cultural contexts. But they claim to characterize these forms of life. in a disengaged, neutral manner that, unless it is surreptitiously smuggled in through the back door, offers no way of gaining any of the "wisdom" Winch (1958) hopes for. They offer no way—almost as a matter of principle—of evaluating the goodness or worth of these human possibilities. Thus, for example, a descriptivist account of the emergent neoliberal system of power and way of life so many critics have analyzed in recent years (e.g., Harvey, 2005; Mirowski, 2018; Sugarman, 2015, and others), colored deeply by instrumentalism, would be of little help in advancing these critiques or envisioning any alternative kind of society. It might clarify further the dynamics of neoliberalism or bring to light unnoticed aspects of it. But it would be of no help in our search, should we want to undertake one, for a "new wisdom of limits" on our restless, ultimately self-defeating, search for ever more power and control.

Philosophical Hermeneutics

The inability to find a genuine alternative to a paralyzing neutrality or an intrusive dogmatism is a major stumbling block for modern social science. Even critics of conventional empiricist and descriptivist approaches find it very difficult to envision such an alternative. One possible pathway out of this situation is suggested by philosophical hermeneutics or ontological hermeneutics (Gadamer, 1989; Guignon, 1991; Heidegger, 1962; Ricoeur, 1992; Taylor, 1985a) and the idea of an interpretive social science based on hermeneutic thought (Bishop, 2007; Packer & Addison, 1989; Richardson et al., 1999). A hermeneutic view, I suggest, provides a way of taking account of the indelible limits inscribed in the human situation without abandoning the best modern liberal values of tolerance and respect for human dignity and rights. As a result, it provides a framework in which the reality of human suffering might be fully acknowledged and appropriately explored.

Ontological hermeneutics clarifies what a truly "double hermeneutic" approach to social and psychological inquiry might involve. Twentieth- and twenty-first-century social inquiry has been continuously preoccupied with searching for the right "methods" by which to do their work. Essentially, this means worrying about how we can objectify our human subject matter so that we can explain or describe it in a proper way, unsullied by our merely subjective or arbitrary values and preferences. We have to get clear about what those proper methods are *before* we undertake research or theory about that subject matter. Gradually, over the last couple of centuries (Bishop, 2007; Richardson et al., 1999; Taylor, 1995) it has become clear that such epistemology is stubbornly blind to unexamined, highly question-able assumptions about humans and their basic relation to the world, their "being-in-the-world" (Heidegger, 1962). In one of the classic texts of con-temporary theoretical psychology, Slife and Williams (1995) reiterate this point for psychology. They point out that our guiding principle in modern psychology has been something like, "We test our ideas by our methods." But what if our methods *presuppose* a host of ideas about ourselves, the world, and the nature of knowing, ideas which might be incorrect to one degree or another but are simply assumed and thus can never be critically evaluated?

In his penetrating analysis of this issue, Charles Taylor (1995, p. 3), a leading hermeneutic thinker, argues that the whole modern epistemologi-cal enterprise that maintains it can establish valid knowledge by certain independent standards or methods, and by them alone seriously distorts our situation. He suggests that we take a "wider conception of the epistemo-logical tradition" as incorporating a number of basic beliefs and values. For example, it assumes a conception of knowledge as the "inner depiction of an outer reality" or the "correct representation of an independent reality." Then everything from finding truth to achieving reliable technology depends, we think, on anchoring our beliefs in that independent reality. But many critics have pointed out that this "representational" view of knowledge or under-standing leads to insoluble puzzles concerning, among other things, how we can gain indubitable access to realities *through* our mental representations that are at the same time realities *independent* of them. Any effort to check out whether or not our representations accurately capture those realities will have to view that relationship through other (quite possibly distorting) rep-resentations, and so on, indefinitely.

Secondly, Taylor (1995, pp. 7 ff.) indicates that the epistemological tra-dition and its representational outlook also assumes a picture of the human self—widespread in modern times but in fact quite problematic—as dis-engaged, disembodied, and atomistic or "punctual." This self is "distin-guished . . . from [the] natural and social worlds, so that [its] identity is no longer to be defined in terms of what lies outside . . . in these worlds." Of course, this view flies in the face of enormous evidence that the human self, personality, and behavior are shaped deeply by their social and cul-tural worlds, long before they become aware of themselves as individuals capable of deliberating choices of values and goals. In a more theoreti-cal vein, thinkers like Mikhail Bakhtin (1981) and Taylor (1991) argue for the notion of an essentially "dialogical self." In this view, the mature human self is very much not a center of monological consciousness, but a scene or locus of dialogue. What gets "internalized" in human develop-ment is not simply social prohibitions as with Freud's superego or even, less narrowly, the perspective of another person as in G. H. Mead's (1934) theory. Rather, it is "the whole [cultural] conversation, with the inter-animation of its voices" that is assimilated and joined (Taylor, 1991, p. 314). Thus, the self "arises within conversation" (p. 312). Leslie Baxter (2004, p. 3), drawing on Bakhtin's ideas, argues that we should not speak about "communication in relationships" but about "relationships as dialogues." She quotes Bakhtin: "I achieve self-consciousness, I become myself only by revealing myself to another, through another and with another's help . . . cutting myself off, isolating oneself, closing oneself off, those are the basic reasons for loss of self."

The theoretical psychologist Brent Slife (2004) advances this understanding of our "arising in conversation" with his notion of "strong relationality." The vast majority of theories in psychology and psychotherapy incorporate a model of what Slife calls "weak relationality" or "interaction," consisting mainly of reciprocal exchanges of influence or information "between essentially self-contained organisms" (p. 158). (Note that these exchanges are largely of an *instrumental* or quasi-instrumental nature) (Richardson, 2005). Thus, this approach dilutes social bonds and obscures or undercuts the more profound and intimate kind of mutual influence and dialogue that form a self at its root. Also, a weak relational approach seems to involve an acute paradox. It must account in brutely causal or coarsely instrumental terms for the development of an ideally autonomous, exceedingly "sovereign self" (Dunne, 1996) that suddenly and inexplicably stands at a remove from such influences and can "act on" people and events in a largely self-determined fashion (Slife, 2004, p. 158).

Strong relationality, by contrast, is an "ontological relationality." Relationships are "not just the interactions of what was originally nonrelational" but are "relational all the way down." Each person "is first and always a nexus of relations." In this view, all things "have a shared being and a mutual constitution" (Slife, 2004, p. 159).

Finally, the disengaged, punctual self begins to look like as much a *moral* as a scientific ideal. It forms an essential part of liberal individualism (Sandel, 1996) or liberal voluntarism (Deneen, 2018) that operates as a "disguised ideology" that inspires and shapes much social science, claims to value freedom or neutrality notwithstanding. Many contemporary political and therapeutic ideals for people reflect and reinforce this profound aspiration to individuality and separateness, even if it distorts the human situation and fails to bring the maturity and fulfillment it promises. Our stubborn attachment to this sort of hypertrophied individualism and autonomy becomes understandable in a situation where it seems to many people that the only alternative is an authoritarian or domineering imposition of moral values and political practices.

Hermeneutic Ontology

Ontological hermeneutics attempts to resolve these problems and para-doxes and does so, I think, to a considerable extent. Here a full-blooded double hermeneutic comes into focus. Conventional social science accounts view social or psychological realities as independent targets or objects of inquiry, whether they are portrayed in causal/instrumental terms or held to be described in their meaningfulness in a distanced, supposedly unbiased manner. In the hermeneutic view, humans are "self-interpreting beings" (Taylor, 1985b). The meanings we work out in the teeth of living make us to a great extent what we are. In everyday life and in a more systematic way in the human sciences, people seek to understand the changeable *meanings* of events, texts, works of art, social reality, and the actions of others. They do this in order to appreciate them and relate to them appropriately along the storylines of their living. They seek an engaged, ultimately *practical* understanding that is different in kind from primarily comprehending events mainly as "instances" of a general concept, rule, or law or targets of mere descriptions. New experience changes the meaning events can have for us, not because it alters our view of an ontologically independent object but because history is a dialectical process in which both the meanings of events and our knowledge of them are continually transformed.

Hermeneutic thinkers (Gadamer, 1989) and similar dialogical theorists (Bakhtin, 1981) sketch a picture of a "storied" or "dialogical" self that partly decenters the independent "sovereign self" Dunne (1996, p. 142) of so much modern thought. The overall narrative structure of a human life may be woven from a number of different strands deriving from involvement in diverse traditions, contexts, projects, and relationships. However, the shap-ing of this narrative is not the exclusive work of a single or monological agent. Rather, it results from processes of mutual influence and dialogue, all mediated by language and culture, between self and other, between the present and cultural past, and even among diverse "voices" (Bakhtin, 1981) and values within the dynamic consciousness of persons

In the hermeneutic view, a central feature of this process is our quest for "dialogic understanding" (Warnke, 1987). Taylor (2002) sketches a broad picture of this pursuit. He writes that in *both* everyday life and human sci-ence inquiry, "understanding of a text or an event . . . has to be construed, not on the model of the 'scientific' grasp of an object, but rather on the model of speech-partners coming to an understanding" (126). This process involves an exquisite, quintessentially human, sometimes almost unbearable tension. On the one hand, we harbor self-defining beliefs and values concerning things we truly care about, in which we have a "deep identity investment," sometimes an investment in "distorted images we cherish of others." On the other hand, since our ideals and our images of others and events are always partial or distorted in some way, we need to not just compromise and get along with others, but to *learn from* the past, others, or other cultures. In doing so, we sometimes incur a deeply personal, sometimes painful "identity cost" (Taylor, 2002, p. 141).

Our interpretations of others, events, or cultural artifacts always have an irreducibly evaluative or ethical dimension. In Heidegger's (1962) words, we above all *care* about whether our lives make sense and what they are amounting to. Developing this idea, Taylor (1985c) argues that humans always inescapably make "strong evaluations." We do not, in fact, simply desire particular satisfactions or outcomes in living, that is, "weak evaluations" or mere preferences. Even if only tacitly or unconsciously, we evaluate the *quality* of our desires and motivations and the *worth* of the ends we seek in terms of how they fit in with our overall sense of a decent or good life. Individuals and societies inevitably build their lives around some notion of what is decent vs. indecent, noble vs. base, or deep vs. shallow— the terms vary a great deal across different contexts, different societies and eras. Thus, we can never essentially detach ourselves from ethical commitments or ideals and then treat them merely instrumentally or ironically, but can only continue the ethical quest that our lives and communities essentially, in part, embody. Of course, our approach to interpretation and understanding may be defensive or cynical. However, that does not mean that we have eschewed strong evaluations or evaded the dialectic of deep identity investment and identity cost. It only means we have distorted the process to some degree and held back from a fully mature engagement, both vulnerable and courageous, in the process of growth in wisdom and understanding.

Social Theory as Practice

What does it mean to theorize or conduct research from a philosophical hermeneutic vantage point? First of all, hermeneutic theorists and interpretive social scientists work from the premise that social and psychological theory and research are "a form of practice." That is, they are part and parcel of the human search for understanding, meaning, and wisdom in everyday life (Bellah, 1983; Bishop, 2007; Root, 1983; Richardson & Christopher, 1993; Taylor, 1985d). In Taylor's (1985d) words, in the natural sciences, "the relation of knowledge to practice is that one applies what one knows about causal powers to particular cases, but the truths about such causal powers that one banks on are thought to remain unchanged" (p. 101). To be sure, natural science theory certainly often transforms practice. But the practice it transforms is "external to the theory" and is merely an "application" of it. In human science inquiry, however, it is common that "accepting a theory can itself transform what that theory bears on." Theory may "transform its own object." In other words, there is a relationship of intimate co-constitution, between theory and the practice it is about. Theories "can undermine, strengthen, or shape the practice they bear on." This is because they "are theories about practices, which . . . are partly constituted by certain self understandings." Thus, to "the extent that theories transform this self-understanding, they undercut, bolster, or transform the constitutive features of practices" (101). They may shed new and surprising light on how those practices and institutions actually operate in terms of their ethical quality or consequences.

If this is so, it means that in key respects there is no fundamental difference between social theory and research and, say, Shakespeare's plays, John Updike's novels, the poetry of Emily Dickinson, religious scriptures, and many kinds of philosophical writing. They all represent in part efforts at clarity about the human condition and to advance our community's or society's search for understanding of what makes for a decent, good, or authentic life. In this view, however, contemporary social science needs a significant dose of humility. Psychologists and social scientists who adopt the outlook of hermeneutics are more modest and tentative in their claims and open to incorporating insights from literature, philosophy, natural science, political philosophy, and elsewhere.

Beyond the Hegemony of Power and Control

Several things about this picture of the business of living need to be stressed, especially if we are to be in a position to appreciate the reality of human suffering and our attempts to come to terms with it. First, this view takes very seriously the extent to which it decenters the independent, monological human person or agent that is celebrated in much psychological theory. In doing so, it departs from what Sacks (2002) identifies as one of the "governing presuppositions of modern thought," namely "the concept of the isolated or atomic self, the 'I' with which thought and action supposedly began." We have discovered, Sacks believes, that "this 'I' is a fiction, or at least an abstraction." Instead, personal identity at its very core is shaped through "continuous conversation with 'significant others'" (p. 150).

The action of a mature self, according to Taylor (1991), is "dialogical . . . when it is effected by an integrated, non-individual agent. This means that for those involved in it, its identity as this kind of action essentially depends on the agency being shared" (311). Similarly, according to Shotter and Billig's (1998) outline of a "Bakhtinian psychology," an approach closely akin to hermeneutic philosophy, our actions "are always a complex mixture of influences both from within ourselves and from elsewhere. They are never wholly our own" (22–23). As Dunne (1996) puts it, human agency is "permeated by otherness" (143).

A modern sensibility or a liberal individualist outlook is bound to feel that this picture of human action and inquiry undermines human autonomy and personal responsibility in living. Doesn't it weaken the choosing self and perhaps even encourage us to blame others for our failures or mistakes? A little reflection, however, suggests the opposite. Hermeneutic dialogue requires *both* profound openness to the influence of the ideas and experiences of others *and* willingness to let one's own authentic convictions crystalize out of the interchange, regardless of what anyone else may think of them. This takes more vulnerability, empathy, and courage in the face of possible disagreement with and disapproval from others than mainly asserting and defending one's autonomy and rights, even when the latter includes an effort to respect the rights of others to do the same. The former, after all, will sometimes involve a distressing proximity to the suffering of others.

Second, this view contrasts sharply with both many modern and postmodern epistemologies that formulate their ideas at a significant distance from the concrete, ambiguous, shifting, life world—the scene of a human struggle that, one might add, is laced with suffering. Modern empiricist and descriptivist approaches seek a kind of detached objectivity that cuts themselves off from much of this struggle. Postmodern theories, by contrast, have the virtue of stressing the deep embeddedness of human action and identity in historical and cultural contexts. As a result, they usually insist, the cultural and moral values of diverse societies are anything but objective and are, indeed, strictly relative. However, they also seem, rather paradoxically, to view this embeddedness from a radically distant vantage point, almost a god's-eye point of view, perhaps representing an austere kind of "descriptivism." Characteristically, such approaches rigorously deny that a culture's view or values can be accorded any sort of truth with a capital "T" at the same time they plainly accord final and unqualified correctness to their own account of cultural embeddedness and moral relativism. This kind of postmodern theory seems to be formulated as if from a very *modern* sort of "view from nowhere," explaining why Selznick (1992) characterizes such postmodern thought as the "wayward child of modernism," carrying its logic to extremes rather than presenting a genuine alternative.

Third, hermeneutic and dialogical views, rather than being articulated from a distance, adopt what Guignon (1991) terms the hermeneutic "insiders position." In other words, they begin to take the full measure of human finitude. They acknowledge humanity's acute sense of "finitude, mortality, and imperfection," a profoundly uneasy position between what Blaise Pascal (1588–1651) called the "two infinities" of nothingness and transcendence which can lead to either arrogance or acceptance, either despair or wisdom (Livingston, 1992, p. 4). The hermeneutic process of "coming-to-understanding" (Taylor, 2002) takes place between these two infinities. We can neither escape making some kind of ethical or spiritual sense of our situation nor fully penetrate the mystery of human existence. Our theory and research findings in the human sciences are significantly colored or shaped by our conclusions, at least implicitly, about the meaning of life in this situation.

Finally, a hermeneutic ontology helps significantly undermine our commitment in modern times to a one-sided emphasis on ever-expanding power and control, including the material success, prestige, and comfort it supposedly brings. Perhaps most of us would insist that comfort and control should not be our exclusive concern, but when they are given pride of place in one's personal pantheon of aims in living, they tend to squeeze out any other goals and ideals.

Liberal individualist or liberal voluntarist conceptions of human agency put the exercise of an individual's autonomy of judgment and choice at the center of their picture of living. To protect this autonomy, any notions of the good or the good life one might entertain are viewed as largely subjective, preferential, and self-determined. No one can claim the authority to impose their notion of the good on anyone else. Whether one adopts a more liberal or conservative political ideology, decides to worship at a synagogue or an ashram, or judges the art of Picasso to be profound or merely clever, such judgments cannot be based on any sort of objective ethical, spiritual, or aesthetic standards. To be sure, this approach may create inner confusion or distress as one simultaneously affirms and undermines the authority of weighty and heartfelt values one lives by. Nevertheless, it incorporates a profound, unequivocal moral norm of its own, namely to respect for the rights and autonomy of all other persons, as well. The moral genius of the modern age, if nothing else, is this insistence on the unequivocal rights and dignity of every person, in theory if not always in practice.[3]

To be sure, as was argued in Chapter 3, there is a fly in this ointment. Liberal individualism involves advocating neutrality toward substantive ideals of the good life at the same time that it puts forth its *own* ideal of a good society characterized by respect for individual human rights and dignity. Moreover, it clearly advances an ideal of the good person who respects others in that way and is willing to curtail the pursuit of her or his own interests, however cherished, when the autonomy or rights of another may be compromised. A principled neutrality of this sort seems bound over time to discredit and undermine even these worthy ideals (Bell, 1978; Selznick, 1992). Above all, this conception of mature human agency places few limits, practical or moral, on an individual's efforts to expand control over their life's circumstances and outcomes.

The conception of finite human existence sketched by a hermeneutic ontology and Mikhail Bakhtin as fundamentally dialogical adopts a very different attitude toward our deep and inescapable human limits. Such agency may be "permeated by otherness" (Dunne, 1996). However, exercising it would seem to require greater skill, subtlety, and depth of personal responsibility than protecting and practicing one's autonomy in the liberal individualist sense.

The individualist outlook concentrates on deterring interference from other separate selves or outside authorities and safeguarding its boundaries. It may cooperate extensively with others in the pursuit of shared aims— indeed, it would be seen as psychologically deficient or perhaps excessively "defensive" in a neurotic sense if it could not collaborate effectively with others. Nevertheless, relations with others are mainly "interaction" or a matter of "weak relationality" (Slife, 2004), namely cooperative or (it is hoped, anyway) lawful competition among what Cushman (1990) termed "bounded, masterful selves," which Cushman suggested by itself tended to devolve into a shallow materialism and psychological emptiness.[4]

A hermeneutic ontology and the notion of a "dialogical self" is distinctive in modern times for the extent to which it inscribes inexorable limits on human autonomy, self-dependence, and our prospects for ever-expanding control over ourselves and our world. In this view, a mature person is necessarily caught up—whether or not they appreciate the fact—in "strong relationality" or a mutually constituting "nexus of relations" (Slife, 2004). On the one hand, they are challenged to form convictions and aims in living that they find to be good or worthwhile in themselves, e.g. matters of honesty, decency, character, integrity, or principle, and not judgments concerning effective means to pregiven or separate outcomes or results. On the other hand, ever-present limits to or distortions in our views and values require that we be radically open to and allow ourselves to be challenged by the perspectives of others, even those we may dislike and disagree with (Warnke, 1987). We are often, sometimes quite uncomfortably, dependent upon others for new learning in the things we care most about.

The dialogical self assimilates and joins the cultural conversations of the traditions in which it emerges. It is anchored in and limited by the meanings and practices circulating in those contexts however much it may creatively extend or transform them. The liberal individualist self tends to cut itself off from history and culture to escape any sort of arbitrary domination and then autonomously, supposedly, devises its own purposes in living in the world, intrinsically bound to no ideals other than respect for the right of others to do the same. The dialogical self remains historically situated but has access to a much richer array of meanings and goods of an ethical, spiritual, or philosophical sort, namely internal or constituent goods as delineated by virtue ethics (Fowers, 2005). Significantly, it regards strong relationality and searching dialogue between and within persons, if practiced fully, as a better way to detect dogmatism and domination than liberalism alone—including liberalism's own tendency to dogmatically elevate its own conception of individual rights and dignity over all other possible goods in living[5] (Neal, 1990; Sandel, 1996). It may take more in the way of personal strength and courage to hold to one's own best judgment in the intimate sphere of such dialogue, where disapproval and censure by others is always a risk, than in the liberal individualist arena, where the autonomy and sensitivities of persons are further separated and more protected from one another. Also, this dialogical path takes more in the way of humility and a capacity for vulnerability on the part of the dialogical self as it pursues its search for maturity and meaning, a search that is never final or complete.

It needs to be added and stressed that this search is full of surprises. One can participate responsibly in the struggle and search for understanding but cannot directly control it or know exactly where it will lead. This lack of control is familiar to anyone who has suddenly learned the difference between infatuation and mature love. Or struggled to parent a child who is much loved but simply will not conform to one's best-laid plan for their behavior or development. Or found that a tragic loss or rejection transforms one's sense of what is really meaningful or important in life. At least some degree of this kind of surprise or unanticipated shift in perspective occurs in many if not most of our conversations about serious matters. Some of it, anyway, is a common occurrence. Our relationships and conversations would not be lively or human without it.

In the hermeneutic view, all of these dependencies, limits, uncertainties, and surprises are built into the fabric of the human situation. This view forcefully pulls the rug out from under excessive or inappropriate efforts to control ourselves or the world and opens the door to embrace some of our deep limitations as keys to meaning and purpose in a life that is inescapably imbued with some degree of suffering and loss.

Christopher Lasch and the Ideal of Progress

Hermeneutic philosophy and related perspectives sketch a philosophical anthropology that clarifies indelible human limits and the role they play in the search for understanding. This conception of human agency and relationality may help ground and shed additional light on Christopher Lasch's penetrating analysis of moral and political struggles in modern times at the same time that Lasch's ideas trace out some of the implications of the hermeneutic/dialogical view for both everyday life and our shaky hopes for a democratic society. The decline of liberal democracy around the world in recent years and the election of Donald Trump to the U.S. presidency in 2016 have led a number of prominent political theorists and commentators to revisit Lasch's writings and gain a renewed appreciation for his insights.

In his weightiest treatise, *The True and Only Heaven: Progress and its Critics*, Lasch (1991) provides a historical and critical study of the doctrine or cult of progress, dominant in American political thought and ideology from the early years of the country to the present. Susan McWilliams (2016) summarizes Lasch's idea of progress as "the faith that we humans can continually improve our lot and standards of living" and that "we should seek to satisfy all our increasing desires" with as little consideration as possible of "natural limits or moral restraints" (p. 12). Plainly, this aspiration to unending progress fits well with the modern aim to eradicate or eliminate human pain and suffering.

In the view of most premodern, classical moral philosophy, of course, this attitude is a recipe for disaster. For it, the achievement of character, inner harmony, or spiritual peace requires placing definite *limits* on the satisfaction of mere desires, which multiply endlessly even though fail in the end to really satisfy. For Plato, the realm of desire by itself is a kind of "chaos." That all changes in modern times, beginning with Descartes (Taylor, 1989, pp. 143 ff.), who saw no problem with the proliferation of desires so long as it was possible to gain steady *instrumental* control over the business of satisfying them. In that case, the more the merrier.

This notion of progress can be traced back to the 18th-century founders of modern liberalism (Hobbes, Locke, etc.) who argued that "because human beings are creatures of insatiable desire, there needed to be a continual increase in productive capacities to satisfy those desires" (McWilliams, 2016, p. 14). Lasch (1991) contends that today both, the political left and political right *share* the same deep "belief in the desirability and inevitability of technical and economic development" (p. 23). For contemporary American left-wingers this kind of exaggerated "technological optimism" is coupled with "cultural cosmopolitanism" and "various doctrines of personal liberation" while right-wingers add to the mix a "program of market deregulation" and an unqualified "vision of unending economic growth" (McWilliams, 2016, pp. 12–13).

In Lasch's (1991, p. 23) view, the problem with this one-sided doctrine of unending progress is that it is "self-defeating." It leads to or at least contributes substantially to such evils and dilemmas as a widening gap between rich and poor nations, flagrant inequality at home, insurrections and terrorism against the West, collapse of the middle class, self-serving elites at the top of both political parties in the USA, authoritarian populist movements in ostensible Western democracies, deterioration of the planet's climate and resources, and pervasive cultural and moral degradation in what Chen (2016) calls "a society focused on meritocratic, materialistic success."

In *The True and Only Heaven*, Lasch chronicles the fascinating history of neglected or forgotten thinkers from the American revolution into the 20th century, like Randolph Bourne, Orestes Brownson, Josiah Royce, and Georges Sorel, who along with others like Jonathan Edwards and Ralph Waldo Emerson, keenly detected many of the flaws of "progress" and a hurtling capitalism. They had little success, like ourselves, in envisioning plausible, practical alternatives. But they comprise a somewhat coherent anti-progressive "populist"[6] tradition of thought, with which Lasch feels we need to reconnect. He felt it might be possible to embrace such populism without nativism and anti-intellectualism. Lasch never suggested that the populist tradition or genuinely democratic populism was the solution to all of progressivism's problems or claimed that he knew exactly how it might be cultivated in a modern economy. But he and others [for example, Wendell Berry (2003) and Eric Liu and Nick Hanauer (2011)] elucidate some of its ideals and qualities. These include more in the way of small-scale production and political decentralization, resistance to innovation for innovation's sake, endorsement of a petty bourgeois stress on loyalty, hard work, and self-discipline, actively self-governing communities as opposed to rule by technocratic experts, and the "pursuit of useful callings (as opposed to luxury and worldly success)" (McWilliams, 2016, p. 14).

Lasch argued that democratic populism would, above all, take up the "forbidden topic of limits." He inaugurated a search for a "new wisdom of limits," one that encouraged more modest standards of living that were in accord with the values of a great many ordinary Americans who know that one can't have everything, that most choices involve trade-offs, and that everything comes at a cost. Lasch objects to the way that political ideologies peddle "optimism" about an unending improvement that is out of touch with ordinary people's lives and fails elites, as well. In its place, he cautiously recommends "hope," hope for a meaningful life that might come in spite of, or better incorporates, indelible human limits. [Elshtain (1999) discusses this important idea of Lasch in some detail.]

The Revolt of the Elite

In *The Revolt of the Elites*, a collection of short essays published posthumously in 1995, Lasch extends and deepens his exploration of the possibility of a democratic populism and a new "wisdom of limits."

To begin with, Lasch argues that we need to update Ortega and Gasset's (1994) famous notion of "the revolt of the masses," the masses being a new kind of multitude who combine "radical ingratitude with an unquestioned belief in limitless possibility" (p. 40). There is little sense of indebtedness to the cultural past or dependence on many others in the current society. They celebrate specialization and technical expertise and are concerned mainly to rise in the modern meritocracy. But such meritocracy is a "parody of democracy" and its opportunities to rise—here Lasch (1991, p. 41) quotes R.H. Tawney in his noteworthy 1924 book entitled *Equality*—"'are no substitute for a general diffusion of the means of civilization,' of the 'dignity and culture' that are needed by all 'whether they rise or not.'" Today, however, the greatest threat to democracy and civilization Lasch suggests comes from social and economic *elites* who retain most of the wealth and income, have themselves little or no sense of history or indebtedness to it, identify with no particular nation or community, and enjoy a "global bazaar" far from the madding crowd and entirely out of touch with ordinary working folk.

Contemporary virtue ethics (Fowers, 2005; Fowers, Richardson, & Slife, 2017; MacIntyre, 1981, Richardson, 2012) may help pin down the sources of this neglect of any more substantive ideals of character or the good life beyond chasing limitless possibility. In this view, we have had great difficulty imagining moral values that might have genuine authority for us that are not arbitrary or do not serve mainly to rationalize domination of one individual or group over another.[7] A virtue ethics perspective, discussed earlier, holds that the most basic or primary kind of human social practice is not "means-end" or narrowly instrumental activity but "constituent-end" practices, in which any action or reflection pursued is a constituent or organic part of the *ends* that are sought, that is, *being* such and such kind or person, family, or community. A great many people harbor and indeed are defined as persons by some such core values, however much difficulty their professed moral or political outlooks may have acknowledging and making real sense of them. These are ideals they come to truly *want* to cultivate and experience, rather than being imposed by some alien agency or authority. This pursuit is typically both more intellectually and emotionally demanding and more fulfilling than the merely instrumental pursuit of conventional rewards and payoffs. It not only accepts but welcomes many different kinds of limits, as parents and friends accept them in important relationships.

The Conversation That We Are

In *Revolt of the Elites*, Lasch (1995) spells out some of what he thinks would be involved in a genuine democratic populism. Above all, it requires the aforementioned "wide-ranging, free-wheeling conversation" (p. 117), exemplified by both wide open, uncensored neighborhood exchanges and the "[candid] . . . pungent, colloquial, sometimes racy" Lincoln-Douglass debates of 1858.[8]

In Lasch's (1995) telling, the scandals of the Gilded Age (about 1870 to 1890) led the educated classes in the USA to advocate for a professionalization of both politics and journalism that sterilized them as much as it reformed them. One of the villains in this movement in the early 20th century was Walter Lippman (1889–1974), who distrusted public opinion, thought the role of the press should be to "circulate information, not . . . encourage argument," and argued that while the public would care about the outcomes of lawmaking, the substance of it should be left to knowledgeable experts whose principles as much as possible grew out of "disinterested scientific inquiry . . . [E]verything else was ideology" (pp. 168–169). But this only means that the public then "has no reason to inform itself about civic affairs" because "people readily acquire [only] such knowledge as they can put to good use" (p. 162). Hence the much-lamented decline in interest in and knowledge about public affairs among the citizenry.

However, according to Lasch (1995), "What democracy requires is vigorous public debate," (p. 162), necessarily and above all with those with whom we have intense disagreements. In the hermeneutic or interpretive social science view (Bishop, 2007; Richardson et al., 1999), Lipmann's sharp "epistemological distinction between truth and mere opinion" (Lasch, 1995, p. 169) is particularly unhelpful. The "coming-to-understanding" (Taylor, 2002) within and between us that is the heartbeat of human existence concerns meanings that do not resemble natural scientific findings nor can be counted as mere subjective opinion or whimsy. They form the crux of our identity but are never final or certain and require correction or improvement from different, often annoyingly different, others. Bakhtin and ontological hermeneutics may clarify aspects of this process and its central place in human existence. But it would be hard to find a better account of its core dynamic than this passage from *Revolt of the Elites*:

> it is the act of articulating and defending our views that lifts them out of the category of "opinion" . . . we come to know our own minds only by explaining our selves to others . . . The attempt to bring others around to our own point of view carries the risk, of course, that we may adopt their point of view instead. We have to enter imaginatively into our opponents' arguments, if only for the purpose of refuting them, and we may end up being persuaded by those we sought to persuade. Argument is risky and unpredictable, therefore educational. Most of us tend to think of it (as Lippman thought of it) as a clash of rival dogmas, a shouting match in which neither side gives any ground. But arguments are won by changing opponents' minds—something that can only happen if we give [them] a respectful hearing and still persuade their advocates that there is something wrong with those arguments. In the course of this activity we may well decide that there is something wrong with our own.
>
> (1995, pp. 170–171)

In Sewall's (1980) view, Lasch saw this kind of depreciation of vital, messy, unpredictable, but indispensable "argument" as leading to an abandonment of its "original intent to protect the common man" on the part of the political left, meaning that that "[f]or most Americans, the institutions that touch their lives are unreachable." The philosopher and feminist theorist Nancy Fraser (2017) documents this trend, continuing down to the present day. She describes a "progressive neoliberalism" that over the last half-century has moved away from the New Deal distrust of concentrations of power, breaking up monopolies, preserving democracy in the commercial sphere by keeping markets open, and promoting policies that protect independent farmers, shopkeepers, and workers, and the ability of citizens to govern themselves through their own community structures. This approach embraced "corporate globalization," deregulation of the banking system, free-trade agreements that accelerated deindustrialization, and "lethal forms of financialization." The result, according to Fraser (2017), is "the weakening of unions, the decline of real wages, the increasing precarity of work, and the rise of the two earner family in place of the defunct family wage." To be sure, as well, progressive neoliberalism embraced "mainstream currents of . . . feminism, anti-racism, multiculturalism, and LGBTQ rights." But it tended to identify "'progress' with meritocracy instead of equality." It adopted "truncated ideals of emancipation" that tended to equate it with "the rise of a small elite of . . . women, minorities, and gays in the winner-take-all corporate hierarchy instead of with the latter's abolition."

Matt Stoller (2016) suggests that two principles undergird any democratic populist response to this situation. One is that "citizens must be able to govern themselves through their own community structures . . . sovereign citizens governing sovereign communities [are] the only protection against demagoguery." The other was formulated by Louis Brandeis in the 1930s: "We may have a democracy, or we may have wealth concentrated in the hands of a few, but we can't have both."

Search for a New Wisdom of Limits

In the last few chapters of *The Revolt of the Elites*, Lasch (1995) deepens his reflections about the "forbidden topic" of limits and the need for a "new wisdom" concerning them, without which progress in the direction of a genuine democracy he feels is unlikely to occur. In a remarkable passage, Lasch (1995) writes:

> As Hannah Arendt has pointed out, The Enlightenment got it backward. It is citizenship that confers equality, not equality that creates a right to citizenship. Sameness is not equality, and "political equality, therefore,

is the very opposite of the equality before death," Arendt says, ". . . or of equality before God. Political equality—citizenship—equalizes people who are otherwise unequal in their capacities, and the universalization of citizenship therefore has to be accompanied not only by formal training in the civic arts but by measures designed to assure the broadest distribution of economic and political responsibility.

(p. 88)

What is equality before death or God? Essentially, it is human finitude, a condition we all share. It involves a wildly unequal distribution of abilities, talents, and conventionally desirable qualities along with all the pain, confusion, and envy that engenders. It is a condition of mortality and impending death. It entails much disappointment, painful ethical conflicts, some degree of suffering, susceptibility to tragedy and loss, and the necessity of trying to finding meaning and purpose in living even though much of life remains a mystery. At best, in St. Paul's famous words, we "see through a glass darkly." These are among the "limits" concerning which Lasch believes we need greater wisdom, something hard to come by in a culture of "optimism" that places most of its bets on "endless improvement."

In a chapter entitled "The Abolition of Shame," Lasch (1995) deepens his analysis of how we obscure human limits and the price we pay for doing so. He sharply critiques the tendency in much post-Freudian psychology, both professional and "pop," to downplay and whitewash "intrapsychic conflict." He fully appreciates the problems with Freud's metapsychology (or at least many of them), including its problematic determinism and patriarchal overtones. He seeks an alternative to partly outmoded Freudian theory and the shallow trends in the therapy arena that mostly have succeeded it, one that places deep human conflicts and struggle with ultimately insurmountable human limits at the center of the picture.

An example of the problem is the widespread tendency "to define shame" as simply "the absence of self-esteem" (Lasch, 1995, p. 198). Many schools of thought claim to bring shame out of the dark and expose it as something pointlessly judgmental, moralistic, reflective of an "outmoded prudery," and only harmful to self-actualization and a fulfilling life. Some of these accounts extend the critique to the wider society and its punishing norms and even make society itself the patient (Frank, 1948; Nichols, 1991), a view leading them to encourage the advance of a number of human rights and an expansion of the welfare state.[9] Thus, they fit hand in glove with the aims of "progressive neoliberalism" (Fraser, 1017). Moreover, Lasch points out, they do a fine job of deflecting people's attention away from gross economic inequalities and the absence of genuine democratic politics.

Lasch (1995) cites the work of the psychiatrist and theorist Leon Wurmser (1981) in his book *The Mask of Shame* as providing a deeper and more credible account of the dynamics of shame. Wurmser finds there to be in many instances of the experience of shame in severe psychopathology to be "archaic conflicts" that grow out of the "conflict of union and separateness," the conflict between an urge to "merge symbiotically with the world" and to "become absolutely self-sufficient." Often, he finds, there is also both an effort "to hide from the world" and "to penetrate its secrets" (Lasch, 1995, p. 201). Lasch writes,

> The record of [this] suffering makes us see why shame is so closely associated with the body, which resists efforts to control it and therefore reminds us, vividly and painfully, of our inescapable limitations, the inescapability of death above everything. It is man's bondage to nature, as Erich Heller once said, that makes him ashamed.

Thus, shame can hardly be abolished, for it is something endemic to the human condition. Still, there may be a way of living with or transforming life within these limits and inescapable, painful conflicts. Lasch (1995) says that "Wurmser pleads for the 'heroic transcendence of shame' through love and work" (p. 201). This seems to imply a "search for meaning" that digs a lot deeper and represents a much more ethically or spiritually challenging effort that just conferring equality or granting or claiming human rights. Without it, neither a durable democracy, as Lasch argues, nor a more credible approach to coming to terms with human suffering may be possible

"Reverence"

The philosopher and classicist Paul Woodruff (2001a), in his widely read book *Reverence*, has explored the topic of implacable human limitations in a fresh and compelling way. His analysis is enormously helpful to us in advancing the search for new wisdom of limits and removing the blind spots that deter a fuller investigation of suffering and its place in a human life. I put "reverence" in quotes in the heading of this section because, in Woodruff's view, reverence has as much to do with politics and power as religion and sometimes transpires outside the sphere of religion altogether. Reverence "begins in a deep understanding of human limitations." From it "grows the capacity to be in awe of whatever we believe lies outside our control"—God, the gods (beneficent or evil), truth, nature, justice (in his words, "conceived as an ideal, dimly grasped and much disputed"), death, or, if that is how one sees it, nothing at all (p. 3). Woodruff argues that reckoning with this dimension of human life is a universal, inescapable task. Of course, it takes myriad forms in different times and cultures. But he points out that people from very different religions commonly much admire one another's outlook and practices, which can't be based on the content of their creeds. It appears that we can detect and admire this quality anywhere.

The capacity for reverence and its exercise is a virtue in just the sense that courage or fairmindedness are virtues. Indeed, Woodruff suggests it is a cardinal virtue. Virtue or moral excellence, Woodruff reminds us, is not mainly about self-control, but is "supposed to be the capacity to have the right emotions from the start." Preeminently, "virtues are about emotions." Emotions and feelings are

> hard to write about, and yet they are what move us most: We hardly do something well if we do not feel like doing it . . . unlike rules, virtues give us strength to live well and to avoid bad choices. Reverence, for example, gives us the ability to shudder at going wrong. When it fails . . . people in power forget how to be ashamed.

A virtue is "an element in a person's character that tempers emotions at the source" (Woodruff, 2001b, p. 3). Virtues are "habits of feeling" that are "harder to learn or to forget" than rules (2001a, p. 62).

Woodruff explores how the Greeks before Plato and Confucius and his immediate followers in ancient China, such as Mencius, defend reverence as an indispensable bulwark of human society, the thing that alone keeps leaders from trying to act like gods (tyranny and hubris for the Greeks), and is necessary if ordinary people are to find a place of belonging in society, with its inevitable differences and hierarchies, one that avoids the extremes, we might say, of emotional isolation and domination over others. He points out that Western philosophers since Plato largely ignore reverence, perhaps because they have so often pursued objective and timeless truth in a somewhat disengaged manner. But poets from Homer and the Greek tragedians to Tennyson and Philip Larkin, and a few theorists like Lasch, bring it to the fore again and again.

Reverence is, in Woodruff's words, "the virtuous capacity for awe, respect, and shame" in the face of what "cannot be changed or controlled by human means" (Woodruff, 2001b, p. 7). In our time, we mainly hear praise of *ir*reverence. But reverence is not only compatible with but often calls for the mocking of pompous solemnity and arrogant hypocrisy. Of course, more than irreverence is needed, lest we fall into mere negativity or cynicism. In the civic republican tradition, any viable alternative to excessive independence or subservience to others must include some shared or overlapping notions of the common good and mutual deliberation about them. Prizing freedom and personal independence, many of us today are understandably leery about these ideas. But Woodruff (2001b, p. 9) contends that we have to be serious about them because we simply cannot cultivate or practice virtues like courage, compassion, or reverence apart from membership and participation in the life of a community, including its ceremonies that powerfully install a sense of limits and mutual respect. For example, you can't be a courageous soldier in a unit of cowards who are unwilling to take risks because to take them yourself would amount to throwing your life away, which is foolish, not courageous. Similarly, you can't practice altruism or compassion among cruel or narrowly self-seeking individuals because to do so would simply be to portray yourself as a sucker in their eyes, and to an extent be one! Without a community, Woodruff points out, such virtues "have no outlet."

Consider the interesting example of respect. Respect "helps us avoid treating others with contempt, partly because it reminds us of our limitations, and partly because it can be shared in a variety of practices" (Woodruff, 2001b, p. 7 ff.). Respect can be too "thin" when it is accorded to everyone regardless of "whether they respond to it or not" or are accountable for their actions. Kant's concept of respect as a mutual recognition of autonomy falls in this category. Respect also can be too "thick," as when it is claimed on the basis of unquestioned authority or expertise. The enormous limitations of all our knowledge and capacities for moral insight make such thick respect a recipe for stultification and arrogance. Reverence in the face of our enduring limitations and imperfections requires a sense of common humanity. Thus, skillful leaders and knowledgeable teachers must extend respect to and really listen to their followers and students, just as the latter would be foolish not to feel and show respect for those in their communities who seem to have greater knowledge, maturity, or wisdom than they do. If so, reverence and an abiding appreciation of our human limitations requires the sort of just dialogue I outlined earlier in the paper, and is an essential virtue for the practice of that dialogue. Woodruff argues that the exercise of such virtues is dependent on the presence of virtue in the community and that we are therefore more dependent upon or involved with one another in the pursuit of a good life than we commonly acknowledge.

Woodruff (2001a, 2001b) also has something important to say about sensitive issues concerning shame. Contemporary psychology knows a great deal about pathological shame and its damaging effects. But some theorists have suggested that in our current society and in psychology we may harbor a one-sided and overly negative view of the moral emotion of shame (Karen, 2003; Lasch, 1995). Woodruff, too, argues that we have oversimplified the matter of shame. Just as there is a mean of "just right" respect between the extremes of bare respect between individuals that keep a great distance apart and disdainful authority that willfully or casually crushes other people, there may be a "just right" notion of healthy shame between the poles of amoral or immoral disregard for shared standards and needy or fearful subordination to others. It seems that we are so sensitive to violations of individual autonomy and rights that we often seem to overlook this middle ground. We are so concerned about abridgments of rights and invasions of our privacy that we neglect to take account of the importance of "thick" social ties which are sensitive to handle but indispensable to a rewarding life.

Thus, the right sort of shame may be an even more important moral feeling and motivation than healthy guilt, because it links us to community in a fundamental way. It is in intimate ties to others or in contexts where we experience a deep sense of connectedness and belonging that shame enters the picture. Or rather, shame is an essential part of such close ties and living in community. If we can stand on our own two feet and think for ourselves honestly and critically even though terribly meaningful ties to others are at stake, we may experience, at times, the kind of healthy shame that comes from violating or betraying our community's standards. If the loss of those ties would be intolerably devastating, our own best judgment notwithstanding, we may allow ourselves to be irrationally or unjustly "shamed" by the community in order to preserve belonging and a sense of security. So, shame opens the door to some of the most painful kinds of human suffering and loss

Woodruff (2001b) adds to our understanding of the dynamics of shame, I believe. He remarks that "Shame without reverence undermines autonomy" (p. 8). In other words, a community or authority that does not respect the enduring limitations of its capacities for ethical discernment may quash full independence of judgment among its members, something that in fact it sorely needs in the quest for a good society. A prominent Alfred Adler scholar and colleague of mine tells me that Adlerian thinkers, consistent with this idea, often describe what I am calling healthy shame as a "cry for connectedness." Of course, that cry will be futile if we have no real friends or inhabit no communities with whom we share "just right" commitments concerning the good life, on whom we can rely on as needed for both respect and criticism. I would add that a greater appreciation of Woodruff's thoroughly nonsectarian notion of reverence and its role in the good life is stronger medicine for exposing and undermining authoritarian pretense than a worthy but too "thin" liberal respect for autonomy and human rights. It exposes evil and cruelty's pretense and denial of ingrained human limits at their root. Finally, it must be said that allowing oneself to honestly grasp the many aspects of life over which one has little or no control exposes one, without buffer or cover, to the wide range of pain and suffering in the human sphere.

Notes

1. Be it spending unstructured time with a child or friend, acting courageously without certainty about the outcome, deepening one's understanding of history, creating or appreciating fine art, doing volunteer work in a hospice, or practicing meditation or contemplative prayer—these are just a few examples—the activity is felt to be good and is enjoyed *for its own sake*, not undertaken primarily to reach any other outcome or benefit.

2. Social scientists are mightily preoccupied with ideas and concerns about their epistemology. They tend to feel that it is only their ideas about "method" or "methodology" that distinguished their findings from unsubstantiated common sense or the sloppy moralizing of preachers and politicians, that is, provides genuine and truly useful "knowledge." But when pressed, they have great difficulty explaining how this is so. Instrumental viewpoints distort purposive human action, the most basic and important kind of which is not means-end but constituent-end in character. Thus just how supposed knowledge of cause and effect in the sphere of meaningful human activities is useful remains murky at best. The purveyors of descriptivist accounts appeal to the richness and resonance of their depictions but can claim "truth" for them only by obscuring how much they are interpretations guided by particular cultural values and ethical commitments.

3. It must be added, of course, that modern culture has not yet found a way to reinterpret what such rights and dignity are all about in a way that disentangles them from the absolutizing of individual rights, choice, and dignity that cuts us off from badly needed ideals of character and the common good (Sandel, 2020).

4. Reciprocal "Weak relational" interactions between essentially self-contained persons" are typically exchanges of an *instrumental* or quasi-instrumental nature (Richardson, 2005).

5. And, often nowadays, condemn any other view as unenlightened, politically incorrect, or "deplorable."

6. The populist tradition Lasch refers to is almost the polar opposite of the sort of authoritarian populism that has expanded around the world and invaded to some extent even Western liberal democracies in recent years. It advocates on localism and an informed citizenry that participates actively in both local and national politics.

7. Paul Ricoeur (1973, p. 156) called this dilemma the "antimony of value," the "central antimony of [modern] moral philosophy." The question is, are moral or spiritual values created or discovered? In Ricoeur's words, "If values are not our work but precede us, why do they not suppress our freedom? And if they are our work, why are they not arbitrary choices?" (p. 156). We can't live with them but can't live without them, so to speak.

8. A series of seven debates, each drawing as many as 15,000 people.

9. In and of themselves, in many contexts, these may be highly desirable and ethically imperative. But by themselves they may be sorely insufficient.

References

Bakhtin, M. (1981). *The dialogic imagination.* Austin, TX: University of Texas Press.

Baxter, L. (2004). Relationships as dialogues. *Personal Relationships, 11,* 1–22.

Bell, D. (1978). *The cultural contradictions of capitalism.* New York: Basic Books.

Bellah, R. (1983). The ethical aims of social inquiry. In N. Haan, R. Bellah, P. Rabinow, & W. Sullivan (Eds.), *Social science as moral inquiry* (pp. 300–381). New York: Columbia University Press.

Bernstein, R. J. (1976). *The restructuring of social and political theory.* Philadelphia: University of Pennsylvania Press.

Berry, W. (2003). *The agrarian essays of Wendell Berry.* Berkeley, CA: Counterpoint Press.

Bishop, R. (2007). *The philosophy of the social sciences.* New York: Continuum.

Brinkmann, S. (2010). *Perspectives on normativity.* New York: Springer.

Chen, V. (2016, December 16). The spiritual crisis of the modern economy. *Atlantic.* Retrieved from www.theatlantic.com/business/archive/2016/12/spiritual-crisis-modern-economy/511067/

Cushman, P. (1990). Why the self is empty. *American Psychologist, 45*, 599–611.

Deneen, P. (2018). *Why liberalism failed.* New Haven, CT: Yale University Press.

Denzin, N., & Lincoln, Y. (Eds.). (1998). *The landscape of qualitative research: Theories and issues.* Thousand Oaks, CA: Sage Publications.

Dunne, J. (1996). Beyond sovereignty and deconstruction: The storied self. *Philosophy and Social Criticism, 21*, 137–157.

Elshtain, J. (1999). Limits and hope: Christopher Lasch and political theory. *Social Research, 66*, 531–543.

Fowers, B. (2005). *Virtue ethics and psychology: Pursuing excellence in ordinary practices.* Washington, DC: APA Press Books.

Fowers, B., Richardson, F., & Slife, B. (2017). *Frailty, suffering, and vice: Flourishing in the face of human limitations.* Washington, DC: American Psychological Association Press Books.

Frank, L. (1948). *Society as patient: Essays on culture and personality.* New Brunswick, NJ: Literary Licensing, LLC.

Fraser, N. (2017, January 2). The end of progressive neoliberalism. *Dissent, 2.*

Gadamer, H. G. (1989). *Truth and method, second revised edition* (J. Weinsheimer & D. Marshall, Trans.). New York: Crossroad.

Geertz, C. (1973). *The interpretation of cultures.* New York: Basic Books.

Giddens, A. (1976). *New rules of sociological method.* London: Basic Books.

Guignon, C. (1991). Pragmatism or hermeneutics? Epistemology after foundationalism. In D. Hiley, J. Bohman, & R. Schusterman (Eds.), *The interpretive turn: Philosophy, science, culture* (pp. 81–101). Ithaca: Cornell University Press.

Guignon, Charles. (1993). "Authenticity, Moral Values, & Psychotherapy." *In The Cambridge Companion to Heidegger*, ed. Charles Guignon, 215–39. Cambridge: Cambridge University Press.

Habermas, J. (1973). *Knowledge and human interests.* Boston: Beacon Press.

Habermas, J. (1973). Theory and practice. Boston: Beacon Press.

Hammersley, M. (2018). What is ethnography? Can it survive? Should it? Ethnography and Education, 13:1, 1 17, DOI: 10.1080/17457823.2017.1298458

Harvey, D. (2005). A brief history of neoliberalism. New York: Oxford University Press.

Heidegger, M. (1962). *Being and time.* New York: Harper and Row.

Horkheimer, M. (2013). *Eclipse of Reason*. New York: Continuum (Original publication 1947).

Karen, R. (2003). *The forgiving self: The road from resentment to connection*. Sioux City: Anchor.

Kuhn, T. (1970). *The structure of scientific revolutions* (2nd ed.). Chicago: University of Chicago Press.

Lasch, C. (1991). *The true and only heaven: Progress and its critics*. New York: W. W. Norton.

Lasch, C. (1995). *The revolt of the elites and the betrayal of democracy*. New York: W. W. Norton.

Liu, E., & Hanauer, N. (2011). *The gardens of democracy*. Seattle, WA: Sasquatch Books.

Livingston, P. (1992). *Models of desire*. Baltimore, MD: Johns Hopkins University Press.

MacIntyre, A. (1981). *After virtue*. Notre Dame, IN: University of Notre Dame Press.

McWilliams, S. (2016, Fall). The true and only Lasch: On the true and only heaven 25 years later. *Modern Age Journal*, 11–17.

Mead, G. (1934). *Mind, self, and society*. Chicago: University of Chicago Press.

Mirowski, P. (2018). Neoliberalism: The movement that dare not speak its name. *American Affairs*, 118–141.

Neal, P. (1990). Justice as fairness. *Political Theory, 18*, 24–50.

Nichols, M. (1991). *No place to hide: Facing shame so we can find self-respect*. New York: Prometheus.

Ortega y Gasset, J. (1932/1994). *The revolt of the masses*. New York: W. W. Norton & Company.

Packer, M., & Addison, R. (1989). *Entering the circle: Hermeneutic investigation in psychology*. Albany, NY: SUNY Press.

Richardson, F. (2012). On psychology and virtue ethics. *Journal of Theoretical and Philosophical Psychology, 32*(1), 24–34. https://doi.org/10.1037/a0026058

Richardson, F., & Christopher, J. (1993). Social theory as practice: Metatheoretical frameworks for social inquiry. *Journal of Theoretical and Philosophical Psychology, 13*, 137–153.

Richardson, F., Fowers, B., & Guignon, C. (1999). *Re-envisioning psychology: Moral dimensions of theory and practice*. San Francisco, CA: Jossey-Bass.

Richardson, Frank. (2005). "Psychotherapy and Modern Dilemmas." In B. Slife, J. Reber, & F. Richardson (Eds.), *Critical thinking about psychology: Hidden assumptions and plausible alternatives*, 147–164. Washington, D. C.: APA Books.

Ricoeur, P. (1973, Spring). Ethics and culture. *Philosophy Today*, 153–165.

Ricoeur, P. (1992). *Oneself as another*. Chicago: University of Chicago Press.

Root, M. (1993). *Philosophy of social science*. Oxford: Blackwell.

Sacks, J. (2002). *The dignity of difference: How to avoid the clash of civilizations*. London: Continuum.

Sandel, M. (1996). *Democracy's discontent: America in search of a public philosophy*. Cambridge, MA: Harvard University Press.

Sandel, M. (2020). *The tyranny of merit: What's become of the common good*. New York: Farrar, Straus and Giroux.

Selznick, P. (1992). *The moral commonwealth*. Berkeley, CA: University of California Press.

Sewall, R. (1980). *The vision of tragedy*. New Haven, CT: Yale University Press.

Shotter, J., & Billig, M. (1998). A Bakhtinian psychology: From out of the heads of individuals and into the dialogues between them. In M. Bell & M. Gardiner (Eds.), *Bakhtin and the human sciences: No last words* (pp. 13–29). London: Sage Publications.

Slife, B. (2004). Taking practices seriously: Toward a relational ontology. *Journal of Theoretical and Philosophical Psychology, 24*, 179–195.

Slife, B., Smith, A., & Burchfield, C. (2003). Psychotherapists as crypto-missionaries: An exemplar on the crossroads of history, theory, and philosophy. In D. Hill & M. Krall (Eds.), *About psychology: At the crossroads of history, theory, and philosophy*. Albany, NY: State University of New York Press.

Slife, B., & Williams, R. (1995). *What's behind the research? Discovering hidden assumptions in the behavioral sciences*. Thousand Oaks, CA: Sage.

Stoller, M. (2016, October 24). How democrats killed their populist soul. *Atlantic*.

Sugarman, J. (2015). Neoliberalism and Psychological Ethics. *Journal of Theoretical and Philosophical Psychology, 35*, 103–116.

Taylor, C. (1985a). *Philosophy and the human sciences: Philosophical papers* (Vol. 2). Cambridge: Cambridge University Press.

Taylor, C. (1985b). Self-interpreting animals. In *Human agency and language: Philosophical papers* (Vol. 1, pp. 45–76). Cambridge: Cambridge University Press.

Taylor, C. (1985c). What is human agency. In *Human agency and language: Philosophical papers* (Vol. 1, pp. 15–44). Cambridge: Cambridge University Press.

Taylor, C. (1985d). Social theory as practice. In *Philosophy and the human sciences: Philosophical papers* (Vol. 2, pp. 91–115). Cambridge: Cambridge University Press.

Taylor, C. (1989). *Sources of the self*. Cambridge, MA: Harvard University Press.

Taylor, C. (1991). The dialogical self. In D. Hiley, J. Bohman, & R. Schusterman (Eds.), *The interpretive turn: Philosophy, science, culture* (pp. 304–314). Ithaca: Cornell University Press.

Taylor, C. (1995). *Philosophical arguments*. Cambridge, MA: Harvard University Press.

Taylor, C. (2002). Gadamer and the human sciences. In R. Dostal (Ed.), *The Cambridge companion to Gadamer* (pp. 126–142). Cambridge: Cambridge University Press.

Valle, R., & Halling, S. (1989). *Existential-phenomenological perspectives in psychology*. New York: Plenum.

Warnke, G. (1987). *Gadamer: Hermeneutics, tradition, and reason*. Stanford: Stanford University Press.

Winch, P. (1958). *The idea of social science and its relation to philosophy*. London: Routledge & Kegan Paul.

Winch, P. (1977). Understanding a primitive society. In F. Dallmayr & T. McCarthy (Eds.), *Understanding and social inquiry* (pp. 159–188). Notre Dame, IN: University of Notre Dame Press.

Woodruff, P. (2001a). *Reverence*. Oxford: Oxford University Press.

Woodruff, P. (2001b). *Reverence, respect, and dependence*. Unpublished manuscript. University of Texas at Austin.

Wurmser, L. (1981). *The mask of shame*. Baltimore: Johns Hopkins University Press.

7 Transforming Suffering

How might we acquire a "new wisdom of limits?" How might we under-stand such limits as something other than arbitrary, pointlessly self-limiting, or wrongly oppressive? Plainly, such wisdom would be a necessary condition of honestly facing human suffering and coming to terms with it in some way other than sheer defeat or nihilism. Is there any credible way, in Sacks's (2002) words to "transform suffering," a path that avoids or transcends what Hall (1986) calls the spiritual poles of cynicism and credulity, both of which involve a lot of denial and are self-defeating in the long run?

Modern Gnosticism

What is the source of the overriding modern emphasis, narrow and uto-pian, on eradicating suffering and its causes? Perhaps it is an understand-able enthusiasm for the remarkable advances in medical technology and preventative medicine that have emerged in the last 100–150 years, tending to blind us to indelible limits and unavoidable suffering built into the human situation. However, the distinguished political philosopher Eric Voegelin (1987) suggests deeper historical and philosophical roots for this mindset. Voegelin identifies three broad political/theological stages in Western history. In the first, the "age of Civil Religion," the gods existed in the service of human cities and those who questioned the gods or wavered in their allegiance to them or the city were subject to censoring, condemnation and execution of Socrates being an infamous example. The second stage he termed the age of Christendom, in which persons were viewed as citizens of two cities, the City of God and the City of Man, as Augustine put it. Citizenship in an earthly city was temporary and transient. But they also were pilgrims who aimed at full membership in the City of God. "The fateful result of this victory was the de-divinization of the temporal sphere of power," a radical revolution in worldviews (p. 107). This de-divinization of the socio/political sphere reflects the arrival of the Axial Age discussed earlier in Chapter 4.

DOI: 10.4324/9780203731840-8

The spirits, forces, and divinities immanent in the natural world fade or disappear in favor of an ultimate reality that is "beyond naming and direct human understanding." "The Tao that can be told is not the eternal Tao" (Hughes, 2003, p. 25), be it Tao, Brahman, Yahweh, Plato's Good beyond being, or a Buddhist insight into a vast interbeing. Now, so far from an essential allegiance to a human city, wisdom may require a sharp critique of its way of life, which many of the thinkers, prophets, and saints of this era and down to the present day have promulgated.

If Taylor (2011, pp. 17–18) is right, as outlined in Chapter 4, typical Axial Age perspectives involve a particular "complementary symbiosis of renunciation and flourishing." There is an aiming beyond life, toward the transcendent, involving a renunciation of some conventional goals and purposes, followed by a return to flourishing understood in terms different in part from those originally embraced. Compassion toward and care of all others are now central to one's way of being. It is plain that this path involves a great deal of demanding ethical or spiritual effort, a maturity that will exceed the capacity of many. For one thing, one can no longer hope to implore or bargain with forces or spirits to escape or mollify the imperfections and sufferings of the ordinary world. It seems likely that this is why a third stage, according to Voegelin (1987), immediately follows on the Christian revolution in the west. It consists of a variety of heresies, the most important and influential of which, in Voegelin's view, is Gnosticism. Deneen (2022) summarizes it in this way:

> Gnosticism was the belief that the world was a fallen and imperfect place ... but that humans equipped with a form of divine knowledge or *gnosis* could transcend these imperfections, achieving through *gnosis* a perfected existence outside and beyond the fallen world.

Voegelin (1987) suggests, remarkably, that the modern age is to a significant degree a Gnostic heresy. (To put it in more secular terms, it is one-sided and blind to basic human realities of embodiment and limits.) Namely, it is considerably shaped by a version of the gnostic outlook on the human struggle. We adopt a shifting blend of attitudes from all three political/theological stages, but a version of the Gnostic sensibility is prominent. Ancient Gnosticism tends to view the world as severely deficient or positively evil, from which a purely spiritual escape is sought. Modern outlooks are not so hard on the natural and social worlds and encourage much less of an otherworldly destination. But the myth of progress and the relentless pursuit of control over natural forces and human events belies great dissatisfaction with the given world and its raw contingencies and disappointments. Technological advancements in many arenas, especially clinical and preventative medicine, seem to support the ideal of unending progress (Lasch, 1991), described in the preceding chapter, according to which "we should seek to satisfy all our increasing desires" with as little consideration as possible of "natural limits or moral restraints" (p. 12). These often remarkable cures and improvements are not seen as simply enhancing a human existence whose many joys and sufferings, gratifications and constraints, peace and turmoil, have been experienced in roughly equal measure from time immemorial. Rather, they are welcomed as an undoing of or escape from many of the limitations and pains of an ordinary human life.

It is a mark of human finitude that there is no escape from the painful struggles and sufferings of such a life—along with meaningful experiences and moments of real joy, of course, if we are so fortunate. That is why the hopes of the best and brightest "exceptional sheep" mentioned in Chapter 5, and the hopes we have for them, tend to crater (Deresiewicz, 2014b). What is the cure for this condition of modern Gnosticism? It turns out to be difficult to envision.

In a fine essay entitled "The Liberal Arts vs. Neoliberalism," the distinguished cultural historian Jackson Lears (2015) endorses Deresiewicz's (2014a, 2014b) analysis but he broadens its application to much of the wider society. There are exceptions. But in general,

> Among the educated and professional classes, no one would be caught dead confusing intellectual inquiry with a quest for ultimate meaning, or with the effort to create an 'independent' or 'authentic' selfhood . . . determined to heed its own ethical and aesthetic imperatives, resistant to the claims of fashion, money, and popularity.

He adds, "In the technocratic ethos of neoliberalism, the self is little more than a series of manipulable appearances, fashioned and re-fashioned to meet the marketing needs of the moment." One pursues rewards that by themselves are hollow and transient, namely the credentials, badges of achievement, and prestige dished out by this kind of meritocracy.

Lears (2015) suggests that a preoccupation of "process over purpose, means over ends, has long been a feature of the technocratic mind." Occasional countercultural protests notwithstanding, it has "dominated American universities since the late nineteenth century and now seems poised to render other forms of thinking invisible." It is not just that "old words that used to mean something—ideals, meaning, character, self, soul"—no longer carry any weight. Even contemporary notions like "innovation," "creativity," and "leadership" that are bandied about with enthusiasm really "lack content," and "where content is absent, power pours in." He quotes Mark Edmundson's witty observation that a leader is "someone who, in a very energetic, upbeat way, shares all the values of the people who are in charge." Any sort of "existential inwardness" and indeed "the very notion of an inner life" seems passé. (We might add that cultivating an inner life will surely often lead to suffering and pain as well as some joys and satisfactions. Failing to explore or cultivate an inner life may serve as a great way to avoid suffering.)

However, Lears's (2015) *main* point is that even if we agree with this account of the "corrosive impact of contemporary intellectual fashion," there seems to be nowhere to turn for resources to imagine meaningful, credible, alternatives. The eminent historian and social critic Tony Judt (2010) makes a similar point. The "materialistic and selfish quality of contemporary life" which "dates from the 1980's," he writes, "is not inherent in the human condition." But the especially disheartening part of it is that currently we seem "unable to conceive of alternatives" (p. 2). Not since the "lost generation" of the 1920s, he writes, have so many young people "expressed comparable frustration at the emptiness of their lives and the dispiriting purposelessness of their world" (p. 3).

The cultural landscape, Lears (2014) suggests is shaped by three—in many ways interlocking—trends. One is a flourishing "postmodern style of ironic detachment" that celebrates "playing with surfaces." A second is a "positivist epistemology" that rationalizes the technocracy and celebrates a narrow "managerial rationality," including the "managerial reduction of education to 'problem-solving.'" Third is the "neoliberal political economy" that in a sense underwrites the other two and "whose only standard of value is market utility." Jeff Sugarman (2015) and his colleagues (Martin & McLellan, 2013) argue that neoliberalism includes an "enterprise culture" that mandates, almost to the exclusion of any others, "personal attributes" of "initiative, self-reliance, self-mastery, and risk-taking," essentially the "entrepreneurial activity of individuals" (Sugarman, 2015, pp. 5–6). It is assumed that liberty and human well-being are furthered by becoming such a thoroughgoing "enterprising self" (Martin & McLellan, 2013). The observations of Deresiewicz, Lears, and Judt indicate that conformity and misery are the more likely result.

If it so desired, psychology might enrich the picture of this neoliberal landscape, which is also an important scene of human suffering of a distinctive late modern sort, thereby helping set the stage for rethinking it. The prize-winning journalist and author Chris Hedges (2009) illustrates how this might be done. in his best-selling book *The Empire of Illusion*. Hedges identifies deep-seated contemporary illusions of "literacy," "love," "wisdom," "happiness," and "America" itself as a reasonably fair, open, and egalitarian society. Concerning wisdom, Hedges (2009, p. 89) contends that most "institutions that produce and sustain our educated elite . . . do only a mediocre job of teaching students to question and think . . . they disdain honest intellectual inquiry, which is by its nature distrustful of authority" and "fiercely independent." They "organize learning around minutely specialized disciplines, narrow answers, and rigid structures designed to produce such answers." This approach creates "hoards of competent system managers," narrow technicians, and hyper-specialized "professionals" who subtly rationalize and overtly serve "established corporate hierarchies . . . economic, political, and social."

Hedges (2009) illuminates what we are up against with a fascinating report on events in a very different sector of society, where people suffer differently from the same underlying moral confusion. He notes changes over the years in the storylines of bouts (really "stylized rituals") on the World Wrestling Entertainment tour. From the 1950s to the 1980s, the narrative centered on appeals to "nationalism," the "battle against the evil of communism," and dislike and distrust of "all who were racially, ethnically, or religiously different." But in the early 21st century "wrestlers play out a new, broken social narrative" that he describes in a careful, partly social science-like manner. Now, for the white working class who make up most of the audience, it's a time of a "steady loss of manufacturing jobs," "decline in social services," "[crumbling] communities," increase in "domestic abuse and drug and alcohol addiction," and "growing class division and hopelessness." Wrestling scenarios are "psychological windows" into what is going on. They "focus on the petty, cruel, psychological dramas and family dysfunction that come with social breakdown." Wrestlers work in "stables . . . at war with other groups," perhaps reflecting "a society with less national cohesion," broken down "into antagonistic tribes" that "cheat, lie, . . . and ignore all rules in the desperate scramble to win." A vital element in the storyline is the failure of the bout's referee "to enforce the rules, which usually hurts the wrestler who needs the rules most," perhaps reflecting to fans the greed and abuse "wreaked by the powerful and the rich. . . . It is all about personal pain, vendettas, hedonism, and fantasies of revenge, while inflicting pain on others. It is the cult of victimhood."

So, we might say that those who are socially and economically relatively privileged cling to the crippling illusion that money will buy them love and strain to serve the system that feeds them such illusions. Those toward the bottom of the economic ladder are not so easily fooled and start looking around for someone to blame and scapegoat, surely contributing to the political populism that threatens genuine cultural renewal and democracy itself today.

Tragic Vision

It turns out to be difficult to imagine credible alternatives to these distressing cultural and moral deficits. It may be that a principal source of the difficulty is the way that both theory and everyday understanding obscure or outright deny what is often termed tragic vision or a tragic sense of life, conveyed by tragic literature and articulated by some theorists and philosophers over the years. Only by bringing it to light may we be able to make progress on a number of pressing issues.

There is no universal agreement as to precisely what constitutes the literary form of tragedy or the broader notion of a tragic vision. Moreover, as J. Cheryl Exum (1992) points out, "reading is never finished" and "these texts remain ever open to new interpretive possibilities" in new times or places when the "natural human need to make sense of and order out of life and our desire for reassurance militate against the despair at the core of tragedy" (p. 15). Nevertheless, there are family resemblances among different accounts of tragedy and tragic vision and efforts to identify their central ingredients overlap a great deal.

Richard Sewall (1980, pp. 4–5), in his much-admired book, *The Vision of Tragedy*, writes that the tragic vision "is not a systematic view of life. It admits of wide variation and degree . . . as Unamuno describes it, it is a subphilosophy or prephilosophy, 'more or less formulated, more or less conscious.'" It "reaches deep down into the temperament" and is "latent in every [person] and may be evoked by experience." It is "in its first phase primal, or primitive, in that it calls up out of the depths the first (and last) question, the question of existence: What does it mean to be?" It recalls "the original unreason," the "terror of the irrational," harking back

> to a world that antedates the conceptions of philosophy, the consolations of the later religions, and whatever constructions the human mind has devised to persuade itself that its universe is secure. . . . It sees [the human] as questioner, naked, unaccommodated, alone, facing mysterious, demonic forces in [his or her] own nature and outside, and the irreducible facts of suffering and death. (From King Lear: "Unaccommodated man is no more but such a poor bare, forked animal.") Thus it is not for those who cannot live with unsolved questions or unresolved doubts.

Exum (1992) points out that several commentators have remarked on our "reluctance and inability to face a tragedy without turning it into something else." She reminds us that around 1680 Nahum Tate rewrote King Lear, giving it a happy ending where Cordelia is not killed and Edgar replaces the king of France as her suitor and that this version of Lear was almost the only one played on the English stage for a century and a half.

Many have suggested that

> The roots of the tragic vision . . . are found in ancient stories and rituals that lament the death of nature and anxiously seek the rebirth of life,

giving expression to profoundly articulated terrors and hopes of human beings inexorably bound to a nexus of forces that sustain them even as they overpower them.

(Humphreys, 1985, p. 2)

Literary tragedy appears "at the mature period of a culture," although "it retains the primitive sense of terror." In such tragedy, "the element of gesture and action is strong, but it is the contemplated and individual response of suffering, rather than the instinctive and tribal" (Sewall, 1980, pp. 6–7). It seems to appear at moments when the assumptions of a dominant myth or worldview are called into question by events or new insights so that the curtain is drawn aside and "fundamental questions force themselves upon us" (Humphries, p. 135).

Tragic Enlargement

At the heart of the tragic vision is a nexus of fate that traps the tragic hero. Every person suffers pain, loss, great disappointment, heartbreak, and death, including witnessing the death of children, perhaps one's own. Certainly, everyone's suffering is deserving of respect and compassion. But the tragic hero is impelled into what Karl Jaspers calls "boundary-situations." At the very limit of human understanding and power, tragic heroes press those limits to the utmost, ultimately failing and incurring some measure of disaster for themselves and others but revealing something more about our paradoxical condition of enormous capability and implacable limitations, as with Oedipus at his moment of self-discovery or Job on the ash heap. Because of this extremity, as the audience of tragedy crosses over into the dramas of their own lives, even if not lived on such a heroic scale, they do so with heightened awareness that they too must decide, act, and take responsibility while "caught up in an interplay of forces beyond their knowledge and control." In spite of everything, they can be "enlarged by the drama of the suffering tragic hero" (Humphreys, 1985, p. 9).

Any enlargement is born of formidable conflict. The highest human ideals of justice, integrity, and compassion for suffering lie at the heart of the tragic hero's quest—"Loyalty to kin, compassion for a plague-stricken city, recompense for a slain father or children, the demands of justice" (Humphreys, 1985, p. 5). Adding to the poignancy, it seems as if the very cosmos that spawns us with those ideals seems designed in ways to thwart them. Our ideals are not rendered invalid by ensuing tragedy, but their ultimate meaning or sense becomes opaque. For example, the deity's questions out of the storm wind make it clear to Job that "human frames of meaning," even concerning justice and right, "are limited and at best partial" (Humphreys, 1985, p. 115).

Tragic heroes, it is usually said, are not only *fated* but *flawed*. They often seem marked by hubris, egoism, and over-weaning determination to extract truth or impose their sense of right. But to "construe this flaw as a blunder, an error, a sin, is to shatter the tragic vision" (Humphreys, 1985, p. 7), perhaps out of a desire to assert the vision of a moral cosmos that is too neat, clean or just.[1] If one does not go bonkers or "tranquilize oneself with the trivial," as Kierkegaard put it, such excess seems almost inevitable. Farley (1990) notes that finitude itself "seems to be tragically structured: the conditions of finite existence include conflict and fragility" (p. 31). Many relationships are necessarily conflicted and important "values, too, can be essentially incommensurate and conflicting" (p. 32). Human frailty and the ambiguity and intensity of desire "compel human beings to act in the midst of contending values and on the basis of ignorance and misunderstanding" (p. 36). The problem is, we inhabit what Ernest Becker (1973), drawing on Kierkegaard, termed an irreducible "existential dilemma," a paradoxical condition of being "half animal" and half "symbolic identity," half a symbolic self that can reach out to infinity and dream of immortality and half a "worm and food for worms." We are bound to try to reach beyond our limits, bound to fail to do so, and bound to distort things and do some degree of harm to ourselves and others in the process.

Nevertheless, tragic vision, writes Farley (1990), is "ethical . . . rather than nihilistic . . . cynical, or resigned" (p. 27). Of course, tragedy raises the possibility that "life is futile, suffering meaningless" (p. 22). But the courage and defiance of the hero or sufferer, like the "tenacity of Prometheus or Antigone in the face of torment and death," may disclose "a kernel of integrity" and attest "to a moral order," seen through a glass darkly, "that is vindicated by their actions." For example, in Aeschylus' play, as Prometheus is hurled into the void he calls out to the goddess of justice: "Oh, holy mother mine, oh light of heaven, That sheddest radiance on all things that are, Thou, thou canst see the injustice of my fate." According to Jaspers (1952), there is or can be a kind of "tragic knowledge" that comes "through the vision of order, justice, love of one's fellow man . . . an open mind and the acceptance of the questions as such, unanswered" (p. 102).

Joseph Wood Krutch (1957), George Steiner (1980), and others have argued that tragedy is no longer possible because the gods and God have fled and we no longer believe in the grandeur of the human spirit or deeds of such great significance. Even if they are right, we still have a rendezvous with the palpable otherness of a world or cosmos that both sustains and defeats us, and with our destiny. In addition, there are considerable trends in today's world that can be labeled "desecularization" (Berger, 1999) and the question is quite open concerning whether or not religious or mystical experience provide a clue to the nature of the wider reality that envelops us and the nature of human selfhood (Dupré, 1976; Freeman, 2014).[2] More-over, many critics find that modern authors like Eugene O'Neil, Tennessee Williams, and Arthur Miller give voice to compelling tragic visions of their own. To O'Neil, tragedy ennobled in art what he called humanity's "hope-less hopes."[3] In his view, "tragedy had the meaning the Greeks gave it" and he "believed with the Greeks that tragedy always brought exaltation, an urge [he once said] toward life and ever more life. It raised them to deeper spiri-tual understandings and released them from the petty greeds of everyday existence" (Gelb & Gelb, 1962, p. 5).

Any brief summary of the idea of enlargement by tragedy is bound to be merely suggestive. For more, perhaps, you have to have been there. For example, Hans-Georg Gadamer (1989) writes that the spectator at a Greek tragedy is "overcome by distress and horror" (p. 116) at an excess of tragic suffering," at the "disproportionate, terrible immensity of the consequences that flow from a guilty deed" (p. 117). Of course, this reaction presupposes acceptance of some sort of moral order that cannot be revised at will, how-ever much it is perceived only through a glass darkly. Nevertheless, if the perception of tragic events is not blotted out and we allow ourselves to go on through the experience, a "genuine communion" results in which we recognize our own, the hero's, and everyone else's shared "finiteness in the face of the power of fate" (117). What we learn is not any particular truth but a more basic "knowledge of the limitations of humanity, of the absoluteness that separates us [us] from the divine." This is, writes Gadamer, "ultimately a religious insight—the kind of insight which gave birth to Greek tragedy" (p. 320). We experience "a kind of affirmation, a return to ourselves," and are "free from everything that divides us from what is" (p. 116).

Freud and Tragedy

Over the years, a number of thinkers—for example, the influential critical theorists of the Frankfurt School (Held, 1980)—have expressed apprecia-tion for the acknowledgment in Sigmund Freud's psychoanalytic theory of the dark and difficult aspects of human life, its destructiveness, tragedy, and debility. They may have been repelled by the rather harsh deterministic and reductionistic dimensions of Freud's view. But they often contrast it favor-ably with later psychoanalytic and psychotherapeutic accounts that seem unduly optimistic about human prospects This tension remains unresolved in psychology and Freud's relationship to tragic vision is at best ambiguous.

Philip Rieff (1966) makes the useful distinction between pre-Freudian "therapies of commitment" and a historically novel "analytic attitude" that emerges with psychoanalysis. He suggests that all traditional forms of psy-chological healing involve a focus away from what one writer characterizes as "the fulfillment of ordinary needs involved with the production and reproduction of life" toward some "higher activity" or good (Taylor, 1975, p. 112) that may afford a sense of coherent meaning in life. As Rieff (1966) puts it, the expression of impulses [is adjusted] to a reigning "character ideal" (p. 15). By contrast, Freud's view of healing reflects an "analytic attitude" that explicitly rejects any such higher activity or moral or spiritual goods, which he saw as extracting a great price of repression in return for little or no psychic gain. For Freud, the ego is the seat of reason, but it is in no way a source of moral judgment. It exercises a pragmatic, controlling reason, a kind of instrumentalism, concerned only with "reducing the forces and influences which work in it and upon it to some kind of harmony" (p. 61).

What kind of approach to life and living results when Freud's analytic attitude is carried through in practice? In Freud's case, it's not so simple. Rieff (1966) suggests that approach can be termed "tragicomic," an original blend of both tragic and comic elements. The "tragic" element concerns how to live in a world devoid of larger ethical or spiritual purposes. One accepts that loss with cold-eyed, unremitting realism and adopts what Rieff calls Freud's "doctrine of maturity . . . with its acceptance of meaninglessness as the end product of therapeutic wisdom" (p. 43). Lionel Trilling (1971, p. xii ff.) portrays Freud's view of life, late in life in the face of much loss and gratuitous suffering, as a grim, irrational, humiliating business—nothing softens this judgment . . . yet nothing breaks him and nothing diminishes him . . . the work goes on . . . This heroic egoism surely the secret of his moral being.

Still, as Rieff (1959) points out, Freud's view does not represent a genuinely tragic view of personality in the traditional sense. The "submission to fate" that he says distinguishes earlier tragedy "means something very different in the age of science" (p. 63). It is not clear whether by "submission to fate" Rieff means something that includes the kind of tragic enlargement discussed earlier. In any case, Freud's sense of tragedy is considerably thinner than that of the Greeks. Freud puts a much heavier emphasis on what Rieff (1966) terms "the control and manipulation of everyday life, the care and deployment of one's psychological forces" (p. 63),[4] lifting repression a bit and at least marginally increasing ordinary pleasures and enjoyments. Notice that any sense of tragic enlargement has gone by the boards. This is why, according to Rieff, the analytic attitude paves the way for our current "therapeutic age" of "psychological man," who "has no higher purpose than a durable sense of well-being" (p. 40) or for whom "nothing is at stake beyond a manipulable sense of well-being" (p. 13). Possibly aided by therapy such individuals pursue life, in one of Rieff's inimitable formulations, as "unremembering, honest, friendly barbarians in a technological Eden" (p. 93).

As a matter of fact, Freud would have regretted this development. He believed that a "'crisis of coexistence' between [personality and culture] was probably a permanent mode" (Rieff, 1966, p. 8). In the Freudian view, little instinctual gratification and only considerably watered-down sublimations are available in the business of living. In his notable book *Sincerity and Authenticity*, Trilling (1971) speculates that Freud may have been reluctant to envision the possibility of greater instinctual gratification or less "discontent" in human life because of a fear of "the weightlessness of all things" or the "inauthenticity of experience which [Nietzsche] foresaw would be the consequence of the death of God" (p. 156). Thus "from religion as it vanished [he] was intent on rescuing one element, the imperative actuality which religion attributed to life" (p. 157). The problem is, however, that within Freud's strictly scientific materialist view of the world, there simply is no way to defend the worth or importance of such gravity. To the extent it is being invoked, it looks like just one thinker's arbitrary prejudice. When it fades, there is nothing left to deter a slide into a new therapeutic age in which many people feel free "to live their lives with a minimum of pretense to anything grander than sweetening the time" (p. 23). Another difficulty unfortunately, Rieff suggests, is that in this new era, even if psychoanalysis has lowered one's compulsions and increased one's options, one may then face the dilemma, of "being freed to choose and then having no choice worth making" (1966, p. 93).

So, Freud's psychoanalytic vision tries to walk a very thin line between despair and illusion, or between stark meaninglessness and ultimately trivial pursuits, with no other option in view. If the argument pursued in this book is correct, Freud's psychoanalysis, cognitive-behavioral therapy, and existential psychotherapy all represent versions an unstable balancing act of this general sort. They advocate honesty or courage in facing up to the disappearance of wider meanings or purposes in a post-traditional world and expect or hope that "sweetening the time" with ordinary satisfactions (what else could there be) will make up for the loss. Many other theories and therapies in psychology, it seems, mostly skip over the unpleasant meaninglessness business and implicitly assume that enhancing things like "self-realization" or "more effective behavior" will keep suffering at bay indefinitely. Few in the fields of psychology and psychotherapy since Freud have taken up the unfinished business of delineating a credible tragic vision for psychology. What most have done, without apparent success, is try to soften Freud's harsh "doctrine of maturity" by brightening up the picture of human prospects while trying somehow to avoid a shallow and inconsequential account of human life. For example, Heinz Kohut's (1977, 1984) influential Self Psychology seems representative of this trend. Like many of Freud's revisionists, Kohut sought to correct and replace his reductionistic and deterministic view. He labeled Freud's model of the human "Guilty Man," who has to live under the domination of the superego. Kohut did not term his more upbeat, humanistic account "Self-actualized Man" or "Happy Man." Somewhat surprisingly, he labeled it "Tragic Man." Little more is said about tragedy in his writings, however. Having given a respectful nod to our mortality, he turns his attention almost entirely to developing his particular theory of human self-actualization, toward a goal he typically describes, of all things, as "healthy narcissism."

So, it does appear that theories in psychology veer in the direction of either cynicism or credulity, or perhaps a dissonant blend of the two. Making out human life to be "meaningless" would seem to be, at least in part, cynical, defensive, and inauthentic. Most Individuals, except those who are brutally destroyed by deprivation or insanity, experience some joys, caring and being cared for, at least moments of a satisfying connection with others, times of simple happiness or peace of mind, religious feeling, the ethical satisfaction[5] of acting with some kind of virtue or moral excellence like courage, loyalty, honesty with oneself, or love or affection, the pleasure of exercising some skill or competence, the gratification of taking responsibility for a job or task, and others. Human life is replete with meanings whose existence cannot be denied or discounted even if they may be overwhelmed by suffering. In addition, many of us figure out somewhere down the line that ordinary satisfactions and successes can't protect us from various kinds of pain and suffering and that heights of power or prestige by themselves turn out to be empty and impotent in the face of mortality, our own or those we care about.[6]

"Useless Suffering"

Emmanuel Levinas's (1988) well-known essay "Useless Suffering" represents a more astute and credible approach to this topic. Academic psychology's neglect of treating suffering seriously is almost assured by the fact, as discussed in the previous chapter, that both quantitative or empiricist and qualitative or descriptivist approaches to inquiry tend to adopt a "representationalist" view of knowing. They seek knowledge of independent realities in an unbiased, value-free manner, whether it be delineating natural laws or describing meaningful phenomena. Interestingly, it appears that even postmodern (Rorty, 1982) and social constructionist (Gergen, 1985) views of social inquiry that deny that there are any sort of reliable methods that can produce "objective" accounts of experiences or events nevertheless incorporate key elements of representationalism. They lay claim to a thorough-going relativism of worldviews, cultural and moral values, and configurations of the self. There are many difficulties with this kind of relativism.[7] One of them is that it stresses that human action and identity are deeply embedded in and shaped by historical and cultural forces and so denies that any particular culture's view or values can be accorded any sort of truth with a capital "T." At the same time, however, it plainly accords final and unqualified correctness to its *own* view of cultural embeddedness and moral relativism, something that supposedly is also historically embedded and merely a product of social forces. Such relativisms seem to view the human situation from a disengaged, impossibly distant vantage point, almost a god's-eye point of view, representing it seems an austere kind of "descriptivism."[8]

Levinas (1988) characterizes his analysis of useless suffering as "phenomenology." But it is not phenomenology in the conventional or a descriptivist sense. Rather than representing the phenomenon—in this case suffering—in a distanced, morally neutral way, it *engages* it in an open, empathic manner, describing and interpreting what it finds as accurately as possible, including taking note of ways that venturing down the path of engaged knowing may alter one's understanding and one's values or sense of what is morally or spiritually significant. This investigation is very much like engaging in a conversation or encountering novel events that may challenge one's current understanding or ideals. This is commonplace in everyday life, although much social science truncates the process or cuts it short by forcing its inquiries into the mold of taken-for-granted assumptions of about how things work (such as instrumentalism) or what is important or valuable (often ideals of liberal individualism masked by claims to value neutrality).[9]

Levinas's (1988) account of useless suffering can serve as the cornerstone of a view of human suffering that neither (1) sees it as entirely destructive of meaning in life nor (2) seeks mainly to escape it or eliminate it as the only way to a better life. Levinas (1988, p. 156) suggests that suffering is a "given in consciousness, a certain 'psychological content'" that is very much part of the warp and woof of human experience (p. 156). But at the same time it is something different, almost unique, in our experience. He describes it as "gratuitous," "unjustified," and "useless." It is a "vulnerability" that is "more profoundly passive than the receptivity of our senses."[10] The kind of suffering he has in mind is "a pure undergoing" that "overwhelms [one's] humanity . . . violently and cruelly" and is "precisely an evil" and a "most profound articulation of absurdity" (pp. 157–159).

The philosopher Eugene Thomas Long (2006, pp. 140–141) helps to clarify Levinas's account of the experience of suffering. Following Heidegger (1962), Long suggests that humans are both fact and possibility. We are deeply shaped by "our histories and relations with others." But at the same time we "seem to transcend or go beyond these boundaries . . . always transcending, moving into new possibilities of being." However, suffering is one of the main "boundaries along the way which set[s] limits to our transcending or becoming." Such suffering is "non-integratable or non-justifiable as Levinas argues." In spite of being a content of consciousness it is "unassumable." It seems "to have no purpose that can be meaningfully appropriated in common human terms. It is what might be called an experience of emptiness or nullity, perhaps one might say of the absence of the gods, whether secular or religious." Levinas (1988, p. 158) writes that the "evil of suffering" is "extreme passivity, impotence, abandonment and solitude."

There may be limited situations in which we "may be led to say . . . that although we would not have sought suffering, we are better off for having undergone the experience" (Long, p. 141). But according to Levinas (1988, pp. 162–163), in the face of the 20th century's "inordinate distress," such as Stalinism, Hiroshima, the Gulag, and the genocides of Auschwitz and Cambodia, and generally the unjustifiable character of suffering in other persons," especially the suffering of innocent children, something more is called for. For one thing, in the face of such horrific suffering we must pronounce "the end of theodicy." Religious theodicies that seek to reconcile suffering with some kind of benevolent cosmological purpose or secular theodicies that see it as somehow contributing to political or social progress in the long run ultimately fail. As Long (2006, p. 142) puts it, for Levinas senseless or gratuitous suffering "is held to contradict any human value or purpose and elude integration within any rational or coherent order." It makes no sense to appeal to "a sense of goodness that seems to have little connection with any kind of goodness that we can conceive as historical beings."

To be sure, Levinas (1988, pp. 160–161) notes the "social utility of suffering" is often seen as "necessary to the pedagogic functions of Power in education, discipline, and repression." Many kinds of laws, sanctions, and inequalities are rationalized as simply part of the natural order or necessary to the well-being of society or humanity in the long run. Intended to make suffering "meaningful," "comprehensible," or "bearable," such approaches instead very often exonerate "the oppression of the weak by the strong." Levinas is particularly offended by ideas that obscure or deny the full measure of the suffering of innocents. Rather, he believes, his phenomenology exposes "the fundamental malignity of suffering itself." It can't be seen to have a meaningful place in our ordinary purposeful activities or pathways of living.

Along with gratuitous suffering, Levinas's inquiry brings to light a second feature of human experience or the human condition in which we all share. Long (2006, p. 143) notes that for Levinas even if we are relatively comfortable "we can hardly avoid the suffering of others," which indeed may be the most difficult to bear, especially "the innocent suffering of children." Long summarizes: Such suffering interrupts the order of our lives and calls forth our love and compassion for others. We seem to be called not only to condemn the suffering of the other, but also to be called to a kind of giving of oneself . . . we seem to be summoned to a higher standard of being, to a responsiveness to the other that appears to transcend any calculated obligation. . . . This summons may be mediated through our relations with others and through our particular histories and cultures. Yet none of these relations seem adequate to fully account for it. The otherness of this calling seems to be written into the texture of our being-in-the-world.

In this view, exploring of the experience of suffering takes us to the very limit of human finitude. There we discover what Long (2006, p. 147) terms two "transcendent dimensions" of suffering. One is a profound and unmodifiable precariousness. If acknowledged, it is something linking all persons' past, present, and future together in a condition that calls for great humility. For example, Aristotle (1984), suggests that compassionate persons incur the painful experience of recognizing that they are vulnerable to the same misfortunes as one who suffers. We recognize that "we might expect [this suffering] to befall ourselves or some friend of ours and moreover to befall us soon" (p. 2207). Fowers, Richardson, and Slife (2017, p. 175) comment that "recognition of the common vulnerability that connects the compassionate person and the sufferer is strangely missing from the psychological literature," something that can only encourage "indifference . . . toward undeserved suffering."[11]

The second dimension is compassion, love, and care for the other, the one who suffers. All are mortal, all are vulnerable, all suffer, and all are subject to what Levinas (1988, pp. 164–165) terms "a pure altruism" consisting of an unconditional "responsibility of one for another." This kind of responsibility is "prior to" or more basic than the "reciprocity" of responsibility that "inscribes itself in impersonal laws" or any sort of political "social contract."[12] It is a call to caring and responsibility that is "inscribed in the ethical position of the self as self." This is what results from the effort to "think suffering in an inter-human perspective" that encompasses everyone. In this view, the frailty and utter precariousness of the human situation (notwithstanding its exquisite meaningfulness at times), unless it is inauthentically obscured, requires profound humility of us qua human. And an unqualified call to compassion, unless one contrives to deaden oneself to it, is an inescapable obligation for everyone.

Now one can agree that humility and a summons to compassion seem to be in Long's (2006) words "written into the texture of our being-in-the-world" without necessarily agreeing with every aspect of Levinas's moral philosophy and metaphysical outlook. These basic realities of the human situation will be interpreted somewhat differently, as Long points out, depending on one's particular history and culture. Levinas's (1997) essay entitled "Ethics as First Philosophy" argues that much of the Western tradition has strongly tended to reduce or absorb "the Other" to "the Same," where the Same refers to particular categories of universality and rationality preferred by much Western thought. As Bernstein (1991, p. 69) interprets him, this tradition tends to be "imperialistic" and attempts to "conquer, master and colonize 'the Other,'" often violently. Intellectual activity, Levinas (1997, p. 76) says, often involves "seizing something and making it one's own," thereby reducing and appropriating "the otherness of the known." We might say that this approach to knowledge or understanding objectifies the Other, treating it as an object to be characterized arbitrarily in its own preferred terms and largely making it a target for instrumental manipulation or control.[13] A good example of this process is the kind of representationalism that has predominated in the social sciences. Representationalism and a predominantly instrumental stance toward things and persons are nurtured by the kind of liberal individualism that radically individualizes the self in order to protect it from dogmatic intrusion but narrows its relations to others to mostly a matter of objectified knowing and instrumental manipulation— all the while, of course, according to the right to others to do the same![14]

Levinas's (1997) antidote to this kind of more or less subtle domination is to open a space for the otherness of "the Other" conceived of as an "absolute other" that is prior to every initiative we might take in relation to "the Other" and prior to any possible imperialism coercing her or him in our terms. His analysis of the encounter with "the face of the other" finds that we must acknowledge the radical incommensurability singularity of "the Other." Thus, "the Other" in at least most respects is utterly different and unknowable, which means that the ethical call implicit in the vulnerability and defenselessness of the face of "the Other" involves a profound kind of asymmetry. In Bernstein's (1991, p. 71) words, "I, in responding to 'the Other' (*l'autrui*), am always responsible for (to) 'the Other' (*l'autrui*), regardless of 'the Other's' response to me." Such asymmetry stresses unlikeness and lack of reciprocity in relationships that challenge any tendency to usurp "the Other" and treat them in ways that serve our ends, not necessarily theirs.

Levinas's view sharply dichotomizes reducing otherness to a dominating sameness vs. a responsibility to (or for) the other that stresses asymmetry and unlikeness between self and other. But Levinas puts the other at such a great distance that one wonders if there is not in his view an element of representationalism or reduction of the other to the same[15] that he decries. Better put, he may not have fully overcome the approach he critiques.

A number of critics who are in many ways sympathetic to Levinas's view of responsibility (e.g., Bernstein, 1991; Derrida, 1978; Harrist &

Richardson, 2011) have argued nevertheless that it is overly one-sided. Bernstein (1991, p. 74) summarizes their main point that "there is both sameness and radical alterity, symmetry and asymmetry, identity and difference in my relation with the 'Other,' and above all in the ethical relation." For example, there are some important parallels between the work of Levinas and the pre-eminent hermeneutic philosopher Hans-Georg Gadamer (both of whom were students of Heidegger). Gadamer shares Levinas's concern with the reduction of "the Other" to pre-existing categories of thought. For Gadamer (1989, p. 280), human agents in the pursuit of understanding or ethical discernment do not simply "seek to establish what exists." As active beings they are "concerned with what is not always the same . . . but can also be different." For this reason, he indicates, "every experience worthy of the name runs counter to expectation." He asserts that the very essence of ongoing experience and learning is to be forever surprised or to have our expectations sometimes overturned. Thus, Gadamer (p. 322) advocates radical openness to the Other and criticizes the human sciences for addressing only "what is typical and regular about human behavior . . . [as] this flattens out the nature of the hermeneutic experience."

In somewhat different ways, Gadamer and Levinas each challenge us to do more than simply tolerate or even respect the other; and both warn of the folly of thinking it is possible or even desirable fully to grasp "the Other" in understanding. Gadamer challenges us to be willing to be transformed by accepting valid "truth claims" of the other, while Levinas challenges us to respond to the ethical call of the other. Gadamer (1989, p. 323) shares Levinas's ethical concerns, asserting that the "claim to understand the other person in advance performs the function of keeping the claim of the other person at a distance." However, Levinas's extreme stance on alterity would seem to restrict the range of important ethical responses to the "the Other." Gantt (1996, p. 135), in order to emphasize the need to avoid domination, goes so far as to characterize this response as being "captive to the needs of others."[16] Above all, such alterity seems likely to preclude or downplay the possibility of engaging "the Other" in genuine dialogue that might be crucial to the practice of compassion. Either or both partners may lack knowledge or insight needed by the other. In the hermeneutic view, "we need to be just as concerned about failing to 'learn from' the other, and vice versa, as about opportunistically or maliciously interpreting them in our terms" (Harrist & Richardson, 2011). Such dialogue, as discussed in the previous chapter, requires us *both* to courageously adhere to our most heartfelt convictions *and* allow them to be fundamentally challenged by the views or experience of the other. Rather than impose preconceived or dogmatically entertained categories, such dialogue represents the most powerful tool we have for bringing them to light and correcting them.

Gadamer's hermeneutics may help fill in some of the blanks concerning human relationality in Levinas's account. Their perspectives blended together (albeit roughly) may provide a point of view within which social and psychological theory can acknowledge and try to make better sense of human suffering. The hermeneutic account of a deeply relational lifeworld is indispensable while Levinas's view of human frailty calling for humility and an inescapable deep call to compassion as anchoring the human condition requires academic psychology to address seriously the inexorable suffering it has tended to ignore.

Secular or Religious?

Both Levinas and Long (2006), in Long's words, find that there is an "otherness" to a call to deep compassion that nevertheless is built into the fabric of human existence. In addition, both of these thinkers also find traces of the divine in our being-in-the-world. Some will find spiritual perspectives intimated by such a view profound and compelling. Consider the prayer left by an unknown poet left beside the body of a dead child at the Ravensbrück death camp during the holocaust:

> O Lord, remember not only the men and women
> Of good will but also those of ill will.
> But do not remember all the suffering they inflicted on us;
> Remember the fruits we have brought, thanks to
> This suffering—our comradeship,
> Our loyalty, our humility, our courage,
> Our generosity, the greatness of heart
> Which has grown out of all this, and when
> They come to judgment let all the fruits
> Which we have borne be their forgiveness.

But does Levinas's account of useless suffering and a call to compassion necessarily depend upon such a theological perspective of some sort, without which his account of ethical deepening and enlargement is undermined or unavailable to us for our intellectual and moral reflections? I don't think it does and I feel sure that Long and Levinas would agree.

For example, consider the advocacy by Luc Ferry (2002), a prominent French academic, of a robust "transcendental humanism," an outlook that many would find appealing. He presents his view as an alternative to both "atheistic materialism" and Christian theology. The former "dissolves human beings into their context," making them in no way the "authors of their acts or their ideas" but "in every respect only a *product*" of material, social, or unconscious forces (134). In his view, many branches of the human sciences practice this kind of reductionism. They undermine any sort of meaningful human freedom or dignity (133). Such views, Ferry argues, engage in a kind of self-undermining "performative contradiction" that deny any sort of "free subjectivity," while plainly exercising just such agency in advancing their own sort of ambitious theory (134). This approach does not thrive solely on attacking or denigrating the many foolish or repellant claims often to be found in popular religion, which is rather like shooting ducks in a barrel. Instead, it seeks to clarify where authentic meaning may be found in a world strewn with pain and suffering. It may find some religious sentiments or values to be worthy in some form but it makes no reference to anything higher than humans that they should acknowledge, reverence, or love. Still, it incorporates something like a degree of tragic vision in search of enlargement that takes it far beyond mere fashionable individualism.

Ferry (2002) claims that Christianity is in some respects a genuine "humanism" in that it grants humans an "eminent place" in the scheme of things as "created in the image of God" (p. 131). However, moral theology, as he sees it, is prone to issuing dogmatic ethical claims and commandments that tend to arbitrarily override any merely human conscience, reflection, or judgment—something he finds dehumanizing and quite unacceptable. He finds certain "analogies" between his approach and religious viewpoints. For example, both assert a kind of transcendence that "connects humans to one another" in a profound way. However, religion accomplishes this, in his view, by situating this bond in a "tradition" or "heritage imposed from the outside," while a transcendental humanism posits "nondogmatic . . . kinds of transcendence" that are so "*highly valued* by humans" that we "can indeed subsume them under the category of the sacred" (p. 139). This represents only a "horizontal" as opposed to vertical transcendence or a "transcendence in immanence" (p. 25), they nevertheless comprise "mysterious, sacred kinds of transcendence that bind us together because they aim at the universal, but also at a relation to eternity" (p. 140). In Ferry's (2002) view, human beings stand in need of and inevitably seek "forms of transcendence in every area of life, thought, and culture" that "posit values higher than mere existence, . . for which at the least it is worth risking our lives," the "most visible and strongest" of which is "love" (137). As finite beings "conscious of [our] mortality," we posit "something more valuable than human life and thereby beyond it" (140).

Taylor (2007, p. 667) summarizes Ferry's notion of a deeply benevolent commitment (that Ferry terms the very "meaning of life") as "the succoring of human life and well-being universally." Ferry considers the service organization Doctors without Borders a compelling example of such benevolence. It seems plain that Ferry's view parallels Levinas's tale of human frailty, the need for humility, and a call to compassion. Certainly, one can raise questions about Ferry's account. Much moral theology in a post-traditional world would not claim exclusivity for its insights and ideals. It would see tradition not as imposed from the outside but a historical process comprising an existential search for meaning, not unlike Ferry's itself, out of which crystalize ideas and ideals that may become frozen in dogma but actually require fresh reinterpretation in every new situation and era. Also, Ferry may too sharply dichotomize "horizontal' and "vertical" transcendence. But there is no strict necessity to posit a more substantive notion of transcendence in order to grasp and appreciate the kind of ethical search and discovery that Levinas and Ferry delineate.

The remarkable life of Albert Woodfox (Aviv, 2017; The Economist, 8/27/22, p. 74), who passed away in the summer of 2022, represents a moving story of transforming suffering, from youth as a hardened criminal in the Sixth Ward in New Orleans, through enduring over 40 years in solitary confinement in Angola, a Louisiana State Penitentiary known as the most dangerous prison in the South, to a much-admired life of service to others and a kind of ethical sainthood.[17] I know of no explicit religious beliefs or motivations voiced by Woodfox or attributed to him. But he exemplified a life of Levinas's "pure altruism" in perpetually confining and often humiliating circumstances. His tiny nine-by-six cell became a university full of law books, read many times over. He won small privileges for all solitary prisoners. He and a fellow prisoner helped set up a chapter of the Black Panthers that protested the stealing of food and organized its more equable distribution. They fought against rife sexual slavery and worked to stamp it out and console its victims.

> For two hours a day [Woodfox] would read about the troubles of the outside world, which not only took him mentally out of his cell but expanded his sympathy with the whole of suffering humanity. He did not care now if, when he complained about his toilet backing up, tear gas was sprayed in his face. Far worse was happening elsewhere.
>
> (The Economist, 8/27/22, p. 74)

Woodfox and his colleagues Herman Wallace and Robert King became close, warm, life-long friends, working and learning together, constantly passing notes to one another through adjacent cells. During their one free hour a day to leave their cells and walk for a small bit of exercise, they "held classes for other inmates, passing out carbon-copied math and grammar lessons," (Aviv, 2017, p. 13), about which they were quizzed the next day. Perhaps that gives some sense of their deep fellowship and lives of service together.

It took Woodfox a while to adjust to life outside of prison. He feared crowds because he felt an attack might come from any side. Eventually, he became a fierce campaigner for an end to the evil of solitary confinement. But when he did so he discovered anew the truth that had struck him years earlier in his small cell when he had read the words of Frantz Fanon: "I feel my soul as vast as the world, truly as deep as the deepest of rivers; my chest has the power to expand to infinity. I was made to give" (The Economist, 8/27/22, p. 74).

The title of Woodfox's obituary in The Economist is "What Freedom Means." His story not only portrays the transformation of suffering into something admirable and meaningful. It also has much to teach us about the search for a "new wisdom of limits" (Lasch, 1991, 1995). It turns on its head our restless search for increasing power and control and illustrates how some of the greatest goods can be found in the most restrained and conventionally unrewarding circumstances. It might help break our addiction to ever-expanding possibilities and endless "progress" as the main or only pathway to a good life.

Social Theory as Practice Redux

Academic psychology and the social sciences generally have been dominated by a representational conception of knowledge or understanding as the "correct representation of an independent reality" (Taylor, 1995, p. 3). This applies as much to most qualitative and phenomenological approaches to inquiry as to empirical social sciences in search of laws of human behavior. Both treat their targets of inquiry—elements of the natural world in one case, meaningful human experiences or purposeful activities in the other—in a neutral or objectified manner. Such targets may be value-laden or imbued with meaning but accounts of them must be in an important sense value-neutral or objective. Gadamer (1989, pp. 275–276) brilliantly traces the source of this state of affairs to the way in which 19th-century romanticism sharply critiqued the Enlightenment conception of reason that ignored or denigrated myth, art, and tradition as sources of meaning or knowledge but at the same time surreptitiously bought into key aspects of the Enlightenment worldview. In his view, "[n]ineteenth century historiography," one of the "finest fruits" of romantic revaluations and precursor of the 20th-century social sciences, ultimately

> sees itself precisely as the fulfillment of the Enlightenment, as the last step in the liberation of the mind from the trammels of dogma, the step to objective knowledge of the historical world, which stands on a par with the knowledge of nature achieved by modern science.

At the very same instant that access to meaning is restored, the experience and action of one contemporaries and indeed of oneself are drawn "into the orbit of historicism" or "understood only 'historically.'" This leads to the problems and confusions with 20th-century "descriptivisms" identified by Bernstein (1976) and others as discussed in the previous chapter. Cultural meanings and values are restored to us and taken away again in the same breath. They are acknowledged as real and important. But considered only "objectively" they can play no role in the search for ethical or spiritual insight in our practical lives.

Hermeneutic philosophy (Gadamer, 1989; Taylor, 1985a) offers one plausible way to break out of this paralyzing epistemological impasse, namely an impossible choice between a destructive relativism and an impotent objectivism. The search for understanding and ethical insight that is inherent in and fundamental to human existence is forever caught between (a) particular beliefs and values that define our very identities and (b) limitations of knowledge or moral insight that require us to be open to ever new learnings. It is a mark of being human that once experience has wrought some new view of things, we simply can't honestly go back to an earlier one because it is desirable or convenient to do so. It should be added that often some kind of pain, suffering, or acute disappointment is often a key part of the learning. Appreciation of this kind of ontological "caughtness" of human finitude provides part of the basis for any credible "new wisdom of limits."

This hermeneutic ontology entails an interpretive social science or social inquiry (Packer & Addison, 1989; Richardson, 2022; Richardson & Fowers, 2010), the cornerstone of which is social theory as practice or an intimate co-constitution between social theory and the social or psychological phenomena they address. Both (a) theorizing or interpreting the social world and (b) practices in that world are living realities engaged in mutual influence or a kind of dialogue, one in search of understanding and ethical insight in the ongoing human struggle. Having said this, however, a question remains. Just what is this practice, what meanings imbue them, what are they all about? Philosophical formulations of the idea of social theory as practice (e.g., Richardson & Christopher, 1993; Taylor, 1985) tend to speak about practice in quite general and abstract terms. Even creative sociological theorizing about practices, such as the work of and Schatzki, Cetina, and Savigny (2001) often termed the "practice turn in contemporary theory," which identifies shared practices not separate individuals as basic social reality, talks only about "practices" in the most general terms. Social scientists and theorists may speak in this manner because they aim at the most general or basic description or explanation of social reality, at some kind of theory or science that encompasses all human phenomena in an unbiased manner. But this may considerably oversimplify the diversity and complexity of the human world.

Addressing the realities of human suffering and its possible transformation shows the need to go beyond such a broad and nondescript characterization of human activity. Levinas's engaged phenomenology of suffering reveals it to be "useless," gratuitous, and non-justifiable. It cannot find a place among the ordinary pursuits of production, consumption, and pleasure, even the (considerable) satisfactions of friendship, love, and family life. A liberal individualist ethic of individual rights and fairness that attempts to govern such ordinary pursuits cannot make sense of or deal with it. Suffering takes us to the very limits of human experience and understanding where something akin to tragic enlargement may take place. Appreciation of the utter precariousness of mortal life deflates all petty pretenses and accolades and links us all together in a common condition that evokes great humility. And we find ourselves summoned to an unreserved compassion and responsibility for others that together with humility seems like the very meaning of life or highest human good. So it appears that "practice," at least in the case of human suffering, may mean following a path of learning and living leading to a transformed outlook that incorporates both tragic realism and deep care for others, for many including all life and the natural world. This kind of path appears to avoid the two inauthentic and ultimately unworkable attitudes of cynicism and credulity discussed earlier.

If the investigation of suffering uncovers such a pathway of deepening and transformation that helps explain why so many accounts of it draw on concepts and narratives from what has been called the wisdom tradition (Smith, 1991; Wilber, 2006), which refers to the claim of a perennial or mystic inner core to all religious or spiritual traditions. These traditions, a number of which have been alluded to in this book, all include *both* an appreciation of profound human frailty and limitations *and* a sense of wider ethical or spiritual interconnectedness, evincing deep compassion, that may transform suffering and give life meaning. Also, there are a number of secular or less overt religious perspectives that reflect a similar path to wisdom, among them the opaque vision of transcendence that underlies Greek tragedy, Ferry's (2002) "transcendental humanism," and Eugene O'Neil's "hopeless hopes" (Gelb & Gelb, 1962, p. 5). As Exum (1992) points out concerning formulations of the nature of tragic literature or tragic vision, different versions of the wisdom tradition will reflect different accounts of suffering and its possible transformation and different visions of its metaphysical underpinnings, depending on the needs and resources of diverse traditions and historical communities. Nevertheless, they seem to share common ground.

Of course, there are many psychologists and others who will object to social inquiry in any way invoking myths of meaning or any "transcendent dimensions" (Long, 2006, p. 147) of suffering or other human phenomena.[18] Such views seem to violate social science's impartiality, involve it in fruitless moral, political, or religious controversy, and/or assert the arbitrary authority of some scheme of values. Of course, they may be right! But that is a matter that has to be deliberated, not just assumed. All approaches are based on some taken-for-granted assumptions that can with effort be critically scrutinized, with unpredictable consequences. Such is life within hermeneutic circles that cannot be surpassed. Conventional naturalistic or existentialist outlooks that underlie these critiques may not be free of the ethical defects they would likely identify in an approach like Levinas's. Chapter 3 argues that they are animated at their core by a disguised ideology that is itself tendentious and walled off from critical scrutiny, typically some version of modern liberal individualism, a less-than-perfect ethical standpoint. Thus, it seems likely that any instance of theory or research in psychology will be shaped in part by some moral vision (Brinkmann, 2010; Christopher, 1996). They are formulated, after all, by human beings, mortal, exceedingly fragile, and prone to suffering, who are attempting to understand human life, inescapably trying to make sense of their exigent condition, full of beauty, threat, and conflict, and discern how best to relate to others. The result is a moral vision of some sort. The question is not whether inquiry in psychology is colored by some moral vision but whether or not its unavoidable ethical bearing with be put into incisive dialogue with other also partial but possibly revealing points of view. Moreover, both naturalism and existentialism tend to portray highly individualized selves confronting an impersonal and indifferent universe in a way that largely limits the understanding and dealing with pain and suffering to simply eradicating or curing it.

Levinas's phenomenology of suffering engages its subject matter employing all faculties that play a role in understanding, including empathy, reason, and imagination.[19] What it discovers and how it is itself shaped or transformed in the process can only be determined by undertaking it. There is nothing strange or unusual about this process. It resembles, for example, what happens to the audience witnessing Greek tragedy, often in important conversations in everyday life, in religious or mystical experience, in the unfolding of a meaningful relationship, or when significant insight is gained in psychotherapy. It is how life often works. Social inquiry, considered as practice, is simply a careful, studied, systematic version of it that often seeks to clarify basic or enduring features of some dimension of human action or experience.

Suffering and Psychology

From time to time a writer puts the experience of suffering and transformation into compelling words that highlight realities that academic psychology and much modern culture overlook or repress. Here are two examples that struck the author as especially pertinent to our topic and illuminating. The first is a short section from *Ladder to the Light* by Steven Charleston (2021). Charleston is an elder of the Choctaw Nation of Oklahoma who draws on his tradition and its stories for wisdom and illumination, a leading voice of justice for Indigenous peoples, a practitioner of Zen meditation, and an Episcopal priest who served as the Episcopal bishop of Alaska. Concerning "the ground of love" he writes:

> My sorrows are like seeds, pressed deep into the dark earth of my soul. I do not deny the, I do not forget them. I do not forget them. But nor do I let them remain unchanged. Over time, I let their pain turn into wisdom, their grief into mercy, their anger into forgiveness. Hidden within me, I let the hurt they once carried become the compassion I now carry, compassion for all who have known what I have known, felt what I have felt, wept as I have wept. The ground of love transforms the seeds of sorrow to new life, new hope, new beginnings, through the mystery of soul-deep healing. . . . I use my brokenness like a garden until it turns loss to gain and tears to songs of joy.
>
> (p. 32)

The second example is a stunning 2014 column entitled "What Suffering Does" written in 2014 by the author and columnist David Brooks. Brooks notes that in a number of recent conversations he had with people an implicit assumption seemed to be that the main goal in life was to "maximize happiness." Of course, he remarks, such thoughts about the future are common in a culture replete with talk about happiness, where in three months during the previous year over a thousand books on the topic of happiness were released on Amazon.com. However, he found, often when people talk about the past it is not happiness but "ordeals" that seem most significant. Of course, he comments (echoing Levinas on "useless suffering"), there is "nothing intrinsically ennobling about suffering." But difficulty and suffering may take one far outside the conventional logic of maximizing control, progress, and happiness in a way that some indeed find ennobling, as in "the way Franklin Roosevelt came back deeper and more empathetic after being struck with polio."

> First, suffering drags you deeper into yourself. The theologian Paul Tillich wrote that people who endure suffering are taken beneath the

routines of life and find they are not who they believed themselves to be. The agony involved in, say, composing a great piece of music or the grief of having lost a loved one smashes through what they thought was the bottom floor of their personality, revealing an area below, and then it smashes through that floor revealing another area.

As a result, people may gain "an outsider's perspective, an attuned awareness of what [others] are enduring." In the midst of difficulty, they may begin to feel a "call." Their response to pain is not escape or control but a kind of "holiness," not "in a purely religious but in "seeing life as a moral drama, placing the hard experiences in a moral context and trying to redeem something bad by turning it into something sacred." They find they are neither "masters" of the course of their suffering nor are they "helpless." They can participate in their pain and distress and "often feel an overwhelming moral responsibility to respond well to it." Parents who have lost a child may start a foundation. Prisoners in a concentration camp, as described by Victor Frankl, "rededicated themselves to living up to the hopes and expectations of their loved ones, even though those loved ones might themselves already be dead." (Another example would be the way Albert Woodfox transformed himself in the midst of appalling, lasting life circumstances.) Often instead of "recoiling from the sorts of loving commitments that almost always involve suffering, some throw themselves more deeply into them . . . some people double down on vulnerability. They hurl themselves deeper and gratefully into their art, loved ones and commitments." Thus, Brooks concludes, pain and suffering can become a "fearful gift . . . very different than that equal and other gift, happiness, conventionally defined."

These short passages are densely packed with characterizations of experiences, human dynamics, and meanings concerning suffering that transpire in zones of living of great importance, beneath the level of ordinary life pursuits of utility and happiness. It seems plain that psychology, if so inclined, could contribute to the exploration and illumination of such events. It certainly can't replace the insights of Deresiewicz, Hughes, Voegelin, Brooks, and others. But, building on them, perhaps adding to them at times, it seems likely it could make a contribution by investigating in its own way the nature, variety, frequency, personal and social effects, and sometimes overcoming or transformation of inescapable human suffering. Just what form such inquiry might take or tools it might employ is uncertain when leading theoretical psychologists (e.g., Freeman, 2002; Slaney, 2020; Sugarman & Martin, 2020; Teo, 2017) are arguing forcefully that adequate inquiry into social and psychological realities must blend perspectives and approaches from both the humanities and psychology, an enterprise of "psychological humanities" that is just now being broached.

The details of such an approach are yet to be worked out. Nevertheless, the argument of this book suggests that it would be fruitful to ground such efforts in an ontology of the human realm like that outlined by philosophical hermeneutics (Gadamer, 1989; Taylor, 2002) and Bakhtin's (1981) dialogical view. This ontology captures and interrelates insights from a number of intellectual provinces. For example, Christopher Lasch's (1995) portrayal of vigorous public debate, misunderstood in and missing from much modern society, is clarified and its importance underlined by the hermeneutic view of the co-constituting meanings and meaningful events that lies at the heart of human history and culture. And the hermeneutic view of how we may participate richly responsibly in "coming-to-understanding" (Taylor, 2002; Warnke, 1987) even though we cannot predict or directly control much of that process fits hand in glove with David Brooks's account of how we are neither masters of nor helpless in the face of pain and suffering that may lead to gaining enlargement and deeper wisdom.

Lasch's (1991, 1995) idea that we stand in need of "a new wisdom of limits" ties together many of the themes in this book. It is hard to see how that greater sagacity can be gained and held on to—in everyday life, politics, or the social theory that is itself a form of practice—without a fuller investigation of the topic of inescapable human suffering. I hope to have set stage for that inquiry and started a conversation about its importance.

Notes

1. Cox (1969) and Humphreys (1985) argue that Aristotle's use of the Greek *hamartia* (roughly "flaw" or "fault") falls to an extent in this category. Exum (1992) notes that "Aristotle evades the problem of radical evil, the role of the gods, and tragic conflict—all important issues" in a critical discussion of tragedy.
2. Freeman (2014, pp. 325–326) writes,

> If Dupré is right, the process of secularization, with its attendant naturalization of the transcendent, has led to a kind of spiritual and religious involution, a turning-inward that may all but occlude those outer sources of inspiration that had been more readily available in times past. This may account, in part, for our fascination with religious experience, especially in its mystical form: modern man feels a strong affinity to the mystics not because he is more mystical than his ancestors, but because in the absence of outer resources of piety, he has no choice but to start from within, as did those who, however faithful to ritual and practice, favored the inner presence over the more worldly sacred. In this respect at least the modern believer is justified in considering the mystic a kindred spirit.
>
> (p. 30)

The mystic, however, is not to be seen as localizing the sacred wholly within the confines of the natural self, at least as customarily conceived. On the contrary, "The ultimate message of the mystic about the nature of selfhood," Dupré (1976, p. 104) writes,

> is that the self is *essentially* more than a mere self, that transcendence belongs to its nature as much as the act through which it is immanent to itself, and that a total failure on the mind's part to realize this transcendence reduces the self to *less* than itself. The general trend of our civilization during the last centuries has not been favorable to this message. Its tendency has been to reduce the self to its most immediate and lowest common experiences. But for this restriction we pay the price of an all-pervading feeling of unfulfillment and, indeed, dehumanization. Deprived of its transcendent dimension selfhood lacks the very space it needs for full self-realization. With its scope thus limited freedom itself becomes jeopardized. Within such a restricted vision any possibility of meaning beyond the directly experienced is excluded.

3. Similarly, the distinguished humanist and African-American conservative political theorist Thomas Sowell has been characterized as a "tragic optimist."
4. A heavily individualistic and largely instrumental undertaking.
5. Something that in the traditions of civic republican thought and virtue ethics is sometimes termed "higher pleasures."
6. René Girard (1978, p. 305) reminds us that "Fighting over prestige" is "fighting over nothing."
7. Richardson and Fowers (2010), and Bishop (2007) provide a detailed analysis of these problems. They include the postmodern insistence that views and values are extensively shaped or determined by economic and historical forces at the same time human agents have an almost wide open opportunity to choose them on the basis of "pragmatic implications," a paradoxical and less than plausible mix of freedom and determinism. Also, they seem to underpinned by a version of the same liberal individualism that shapes other psychological theories, even though such moral outlooks are supposed to be considered as thoroughly optional and relative.
8. Much would be *post*modern theory seems to be formulated as if from a very modern sort of "view from nowhere," explaining why Selznick (1992) characterizes much postmodern thought as the "wayward child of modernism," carrying its logic to extremes rather than presenting a genuine alternative.
9. This abridgment or distortion of inquiry results from exercising a special capacity for abstraction, prominent and productive in the natural sciences. It tries as much as possible to ignore or abstract away from "subject-related qualities" or most of the meanings of things and human relationships in ordinary experience. One takes such an objectifying stance in order to "regard the world as it is independently of the meanings it might have for human subjects, or of how it figures in their experience" (Taylor, 1985a, p. 31). Obviously this approach has proved its mettle in modern science and its powerful applications. However, there is no good reason to deny the validity of other *kinds* of interpretations of our experience and events, reflecting different *ways* of being involved with the world. Such a "spectator" view of knowing (Slife & Williams, 1995) is impotent or harmful, for example, in appreciating beauty in nature or art or seeking to understand the needs or distress of a child in one's care.

10. The receptivity of our senses, Levinas writes, is "already the activity of welcome, and straight away becomes perception," something that usually fits in with our ongoing purposeful activity.

11. There are a few studies that explore the response of more or less compassionate individuals to the suffering of others (e.g., Goetz, Keltner, & Simon-Thomas, 2010; Oveis, Horberg, & Keltner, 2010; Rudolph, Roesch, Greitemeyer, & Weiner, 2004). They obtain results showing such things as that compassion responses are more likely when the sufferer is vulnerable or has less control over the problem. But they don't discuss the fundamental commonality of human suffering as a deeper ethical or existential matter.

12. Such "reciprocity" would appear to be essentially the sort of mutual acknowledgement of human rights or liberal individualism, discussed in Chapter 3, that provides the ethical underpinnings or "disguised ideology" of much modern social science. Even if this view reflects important ethical ideals, it does not get to the bottom of our great vulnerability and deeper links and obligations to one another.

13. The theoretical psychologist Vandenberg (1999) concurs with Levinas that "much of Western philosophy has been structured by Greek concerns with epistemology, rationality, and the pursuit of truth," the sort of truth that "is achieved through classification, generalization, [and] extracting the essential features of objects and events that endure across points in time" (p. 33). Even Husserl and Heidegger, whose work in the tradition of phenomenology and existentialism Levinas builds on, failed in Vandenberg's view to fully "appreciate the fundamentally social, and therefore ethical nature of human existence."

14. As discussed in Chapter 3, notwithstanding a sincere attempt rescue morality from a severe anti-authoritarianism, liberal individualism may harbor internal contradictions that cause it to unravel and undermine its own best values of human rights and dignity. A hyper-competitive neoliberalism would seem almost inevitably to ensue.

15. In other words, a great distance between self and other means that little can be said about either one other than that, in the same way, they cannot be prejudged or known by the other.

16. In this article, Gantt (1996) goes on to say the relation between the agent and object of compassion is also "covenantal" but does not spell out what this might mean for a greater reciprocity between self and other in this article. However, he does much of that in later writings and modifies his view (e.g., Williams & Gantt, 2002).

17. In 1972, already in prison, Woodfox was charged, based on no evidence other than his recent association with the Black Panthers, with the murder of a prison guard. In 2014 the US Court of appeals overturned his conviction at age 69, citing racism.

18. I say this based partly on many conversations with colleagues and graduate students in psychology over the years. Many plainly insist on a firm naturalism that seems to them to be the only effective antidote to dogmatism and breaches of individual liberty or rights. The views of some seem also to be colored by existentialism. I remember well when a graduate student, one of the brightest in her class, burst out with that acclamation that "Only when you grasp the complete meaninglessness of human existence can your life for the first time be flooded with meaning!" Some do come around for the first time to see the arbitrary and perhaps semi-dogmatic aspect of their own approach. Of course,

there is always the possibility that their teacher influenced them unduly. But it seemed like genuine discovery.

19. The theoretical psychologist Mark Freeman (2022, p. 343) recently has argued for an approach to inquiry similar to the one sketched here. In a chapter summarizing "narrative psychology," an approach akin to philosophical hermeneutics and interpretive social science, Freeman suggests that in order to do its job well narrative psychology must fulfill an "ethical requirement." In order to adequately portray "the other's lived reality," the theorist must not only approach human experience and social reality with "fundamental *respect* for humanity" but with "empathy, care . . . and *compassion.*" "Relating to its subject matter in this way," he suggests, often brings about a certain "enlargement."

References

Aviv, R. (2017, January 16). How Albert Woodfox survived solitary. *The New Yorker.* Retrieved from www.newyorker.com/magazine/2017/01/16/how-albertwoodfox-survived-solitary

(Anonymous). (2022, August 27). What freedom means. *The Economist,* 74.

Aristotle. (1984). *The Complete works of Aristotle: The revised Oxford translation* (J. Barnes, Ed.). Princeton, N. J.: Princeton University Press.

Aviv, R. (2017, January 16). How Albert Woodfox survived solitary. *The New Yorker.* Retrieved from www.newyorker.com/magazine/2017/01/16/how-albert-woodfox-survved-solitary

Bakhtin, M. (1981). *The dialogic imagination.* Austin, TX: University of Texas Press.

Becker, E. (1973). *The denial of death.* New York: Free Press.

Berger, P. (1999). *The desecularization of the world: Resurgent religion and world politics.* Grand Rapids, MI.: William B. Eerdmans Publishing Co.

Bernstein, R. (1991). Incommensurability and otherness revisited. In E. Deutsch (Ed.), *Culture and modernity: East-West philosophic perspectives* (pp. 85–103). Honolulu: University of Hawaii Press.

Bernstein, R. J. (1976). *The restructuring of social and political theory.* Philadelphia: University of Pennsylvania Press.

Bishop, Robert C. (2007). *The Philosophy of the Social Sciences: An Introduction.* New York: Continuum.

Brooks, D. (2014, April 8). What suffering does. *The New York Times,* A25.

Brinkman, S. (2010). *Perspectives on normativity.* New York: Springer.

Charleston, S. (2021). *Ladder to the light.* Minneapolis: Broadleaf Books.

Christopher, J. (1996). Counseling's inescapable moral visions. *Journal of Counseling & Development, 75,* 17–25.

Cox, R. (1969). *Between heaven and earth: Shakespeare, Dostoevsky, and the meaning of Christian tragedy.* New York: Holt, Rinehart and Winston.

Deneen, P. (2022, March 2). Russia, America, and the danger of Political Gnosticism. *The Postliberal Order.* Retrieved from https://postliberalorder.substack.com

Deresiewicz, W. (2014a, July). Don't send your kid to the Ivy League. *The New Republic.* Retrieved from https://newrepublic.com/article/118747/ivy-league-schools-are-overrated-send-your-kids-elsewhere

Deresiewicz, W. (2014b). *Excellent sheep: The miseducation of the American elite.* New York: The Free Press.

Derrida, J. (1978). Violence and metaphysics: An essay on the thought of Emmanuel Levinas. In A. Bass (Trans.), *Writing and difference.* Chicago: University of Chicago Press.

Dupré, L. (1976). *Transcendent selfhood: The rediscovery of the inner life.* New York: Seabury Press.

Exum, J. (1992). *Tragedy and biblical narrative: Arrows of the almighty.* Cambridge: Cambridge University Press.

Farley, W. (1990). *Tragic vision and divine compassion.* Louisville, KY: Westminster/John Knox Press.

Ferry, L. (2002). *Man made God: The meaning of life* (D. Pellauer, Trans.). Chicago & London: University of Chicago Press.

Fowers, B., Richardson, F., & Slife, B. (2017). *Frailty, suffering, and vice: Flourishing in the face of human limitations.* Washington, DC: American Psychological Association Press Books.

Freeman, M. (2002). Narrative psychology and beyond: Returning the other to the story of the self. In B. Slife, S. Yanchar, & F. Richardson (Eds.), *Routledge international handbook of theoretical and philosophical psychology* (pp. 330–346). New York: Routledge.

Freeman, M. (2014). Listening to the claims of experience: Psychology and the question of transcendence. *Pastoral Psychology, 63,* 323–337.

Gadamer, H.-G. (1989). *Truth and method, second revised edition* (J. Weinsheimer & D. Marshall, Trans.). New York: Crossroad.

Gantt, E.E. (1996). Social Constructionism and the ethics of hedonism. *Journal of Theoretical and Philosophical Psychology, 16,* 123–140.

Gantt, E., & Williams, R. (2002). *Psychology for the Other: Levinas, Ethics and the Practice of Psychology.* New York: Routledge.

Gelb, A., & Gelb, B. (1962). *O'Neill.* New York: Harper and Row.

Gergen, K. (1985). The social constructionist movement in modern psychology. *American Psychologist, 40,* 266–275.

Girard, R. (1978). *Things hidden since the foundation of the world.* Stanford: Stanford University Press.

Goetz, J., Keltner, D., & Simon-Thomas, E. (2010). Compassion: An evolutionary analysis and empirical review. *Psychological Bulletin, 136,* 351–374. http://doi.org/10.1037/a0018807

Hall, D. (1986). *God and human suffering: An exercise in the theology of the cross.* Minneapolis, MN: Augsburg Publishing House.

Harrist, S., & Richardson, F. (2011). Levinas and hermeneutics on ethics and the other. *Journal of Theoretical and Philosophical Psychology, 22,* 342–358.

Hedges, C. (2009). *Empire of illusion: The end of literacy and the triumph of spectacle.* New York: Nation Books.

Heidegger, M. (1962). *Being and time.* New York: Harper & Row.

Held, D. (1980). *Introduction to critical theory: Horkheimer to Habermas.* Berkeley, CA: University of California Press.

Hughes, G. (2003). *Transcendence and history: The search for ultimacy from ancient societies to postmodernity.* Columbia, MO: Missouri University Press.

Humphreys, W. (1985). *The tragic vision and the Hebrew tradition.* Eugene, OR: Wipf and Stock Publishers.

Jaspers, K. (1952). *The origin and goal of history* (p. 215). London: Routledge and Kegan Paul.

Judt, T. (2010). *Ill fares the land.* New York: Penguin.

Kohut, H. (1977). *The restoration of the self.* New York: International Universities Press, Inc.

Kohut, H. (1984). *How does analysis cure?* New York: Norton.

Krutch, J. (1957). *The modern temper.* New York: Harcourt, Brace and World.

Lasch, C. (1991). *The true and only heaven: Progress and its critics.* New York: W. W. Norton.

Lasch, C. (1995). *The revolt of the elites and the betrayal of democracy.* New York: W. W. Norton.

Lears, J. (2015, April 20). The liberal arts vs. Neoliberalism. *Commonweal Magazine.*

Levinas, E. (1988). Useless suffering. In R. Bernasconi & D. Woods (Eds.), *The provocation of Levinas* (pp. 156–167). London: Routledge.

Levinas, E. (1997). Ethics as first philosophy. In S. Hand (Ed.), *The Levinas reader* (pp. 76–87, S. Hand & M. Temple, Trans.). Malden, MA: Blackwell Publishers, Inc.

Long, E. (2006). Suffering and transcendence. *International Journal of the Philosophy of Religion, 60,* 139–148.

Martin, J., & McLellan, A. (2013). *The education of selves: How psychology transformed students.* New York: Oxford University Press.

Oveis, C., Horberg, E., & Keltner, D. (2010). Compassion, pride, and social intuitions of self-other similarity. *Journal of Social and Personality Psychology, 98,* 618–630. http://doi.org/10.1037/a0017628

Packer, M., & Addison, R. (1989). *Entering the circle: Hermeneutic investigation in psychology.* Albany, NY: SUNY Press.

Richardson, F. (2022). Philosophical hermeneutics: Beyond objectivism and relativism. In B. Slife, S. Yanchar, & F. Richardson (Eds.), *Routledge international handbook of theoretical and philosophical psychology* (pp. 111–129). New York: Routledge.

Richardson, F., & Christopher, J. (1993). Social theory as practice: Metatheoretical options for social inquiry. *Journal of Theoretical and Philosophical Psychology, 13*(2), 137–153.

Richardson, F., and Fowers, B. (2010). Hermeneutics and Sociocultural Perspectives in Psychology. In S. Kirschner & J. Martin (Eds.). *The Sociocultural Turn in Psychology: Contemporary Perspectives on the Contextual Emergence of Mind and Self.* New York: Columbia University Press.

Rieff, P. (1959). *Freud: The mind of a moralist.* Chicago: University of Chicago Press.

Rieff, P. (1966). *The triumph of the therapeutic.* New York: Harper.

Rorty, R. (1982). *Consequences of pragmatism.* Minneapolis, MN: University of Minnesota Press.

Rudolph, U., Roesch, S., Greitemeyer, T., & Weiner, B. (2004). A meta-analytic review of help giving and aggression from an attributional perspective: Contributions to a general theory of motivation. *Cognition and Emotion, 18,* 815–848. htpp://doi.org/10.1080/02699930341000248

Sacks, J. (2002). *The dignity of difference: How to avoid the clash of civilizations.* London: Continuum.

Schatzki, T., Cetina, K., & von Savigny, E. (Eds.). (2001). *The practice turn in contemporary theory*. London: Routledge.

Selznick, Philip. (1992). *The Moral Commonwealth: Social Theory and the Promise of Community.* Berkeley: University of California Press.

Sewall, R. (1980). *The vision of tragedy*. New Haven, CT: Yale University Press.

Slaney, K. (2020). The message in the medium: Knowing the psychological through art. In J. Sugarman & J. Martin (Eds.), *A humanities approach to the psychology of personhood* (pp. 8–29). New York: Routledge.

Smith, H. (1991). *The world's religions*. San Francisco: HarperCollins.

Slife, B., and Williams, R. (1995). *What's behind the research? Discovering hidden assumptions in the behavioral sciences*. Thousand Oaks, CA: SAGE Publications.

Steiner, G. (1980). *The death of tragedy*. New York: Oxford University Press.

Sugarman, J. (2015). Neoliberalism and psychological ethics. *Journal of Theoretical and Philosophical Psychology*, *35*, 103–116.

Sugarman, J., & Martin, J. (2020). *A humanities approach to the psychology of personhood* (pp. 8–29). New York: Routledge.

Taylor, C. (1975). *Hegel*. Cambridge: Cambridge University Press.

Taylor, C. (1985). Social theory as practice. In *Philosophy and the human sciences: Philosophical papers* (Vol. 2). Cambridge: Cambridge University Press.

Taylor, C. (1985a). *Philosophy and the human sciences: Philosophical papers* (Vol. 2). Cambridge: Cambridge University Press.

Taylor, Charles. (1985b). Self-Interpreting Animals. *In Human Agency and Language: Philosophical Papers*, Vol. 1, 45–76. Cambridge: Cambridge University Press.

Taylor, Charles. (1985c). What Is Human Agency. *In Human Agency and Language: Philosophical Papers*, Vol. 1, 15–44. Cambridge: Cambridge University Press.

Taylor, Charles. (1985d). Social Theory as Practice. *In Philosophy and the Human Sciences: Philosophical Papers*, Vol. 2, 91–115. Cambridge: Cambridge University Press.

Taylor, C. (1995). *Philosophical arguments*. Cambridge, MA: Harvard. University Press.

Taylor, C. (2002). Gadamer and the human sciences. In R. Dostal (Ed.), *The Cambridge companion to Gadamer* (pp. 126–142). Cambridge: Cambridge University Press.

Taylor, C. (2007). *A secular age*. Cambridge, MA: Belknap Press of Harvard University Press.

Taylor, C. (2011). *Dilemmas and connections: Selected essays*. Cambridge, MA: Belknap Press of Harvard University Press.

Teo, T. (2017). From psychological science to the psychological humanities. Building a general theory of subjectivity. *Review of General Psychology*, *21*, 281–291.

Trilling, L. (1971). *Sincerity and authenticity*. Cambridge, MA: Harvard University Press.

Vandenberg, B. (1999). Levinas and the ethical context of human development. *Human Development*, *42*, 31–44.

Voegelin, E. (1987). *The new science of politics: An introduction*. Chicago: The University of Chicago Press.

Warnke, G. (1987). *Gadamer: Hermeneutics, tradition, and reason*. Stanford: Stanford University Press.

Wilber, Ken. (2006). Integral methodological pluralism. In: *Integral Spirituality: A Startling New Role for Religion in the Modern and Postmodern World*. Boston, MA: Shambhala.

Index

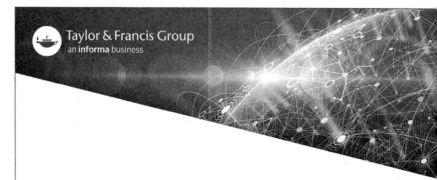

Printed in the United States
by Baker & Taylor Publisher Services